POLLUTION
AND THE
POWERLESS

POLLUTION
AND THE
POWERLESS

The Environmental
Justice Movement

by Kathlyn Gay

An Impact Book
FRANKLIN WATTS
New York / Chicago / London / Toronto / Sydney

Frontispiece. A garbage incinerator overlooks
Mt. Zion Cemetery in Queens County, New York City.

Photographs copyright © Impact Visuals, Inc.: pp. 2, 34, 62 (all Kirk
Condyles), 10 (Jim Tynan), 53 (Piet van Lier), 56 (F. M. Kearney), 68
(Sharon Stewart), 84 (John W. Emmons), 107 (Jerome Friar); AP/Wide
World Photos: pp. 22, 30, 44; UPI/Bettmann: pp. 46, 48; Photo Researchers,
Inc.: pp. 65 (Jim Dixon), 76 (Joe Munroe).

Library of Congress Cataloging-in-Publication Data

Gay, Kathlyn.
Pollution and the powerless : the environmental justice movement /
by Kathlyn Gay.
p. cm.—(An Impact book)
Includes bibliographical references and index.
ISBN 0-531-11190-3 (lib. bdg.)
1. Environmental policy—United States—Juvenile literature.
2. Environmental responsibility—United States—Juvenile literature.
3. Discrimination—United States—Juvenile literature. 4. Social
justice—United States—Juvenile literature. 5. NIMBY syndrome—
United States—Juvenile literature. [1. Environmental policy.
2. Environmental protection. 3. Discrimination.] I. Title.
HC110.E5G39 1994
363.7'008'693—dc20   94-21703 CIP AC

CONTENTS

1
WHAT IS ENVIRONMENTAL RACISM?

*I*n a neighborhood of southeast Chicago sits a group of public housing buildings called Altgeld Gardens. But the people who live there see nothing gardenlike about the surrounding landscape. Instead they have labeled the housing complex "the toxic doughnut." It is encircled by hundreds of sources of toxic chemicals that are thought to be responsible for the high levels of cancer, respiratory problems, birth defects, and infant mortality among the ten thousand residents of Altgeld Gardens.

The sources of pollutants include steel mills and old factories that spew heavy smoke and contaminants into the air. A fetid sewage plant wafts its stench throughout the area. Paint manufacturers and metal-plating shops line the foul-smelling Little Calumet River, which is laced with oily slime. Steel slag beds, a contaminated lagoon, over one hundred abandoned toxic waste disposal sites, a gigantic chemical waste incinerator, and trash-covered roadsides and lots are all part of the grim scene. Many wonder why public housing was built in such an area in the first place and why those producing the contaminants have done little if anything to clean up the place.

Although the Altgeld Gardens area is one of the most contaminated urban zones in the United States, it is not alone. Across the nation, impoverished urban and rural communities have become sites for factories that release toxic materials into the air, land, and water, and those same communities have become dumping grounds for all types of waste. As the international environmental group Greenpeace noted: "Being poor in America means breathing foul air, working filthy jobs, and living next to toxic waste landfills and incinerators."[1]

But poverty is not the only factor that determines whether people will be victims of pollution. Over the past few years, some civil rights organizations and environmental groups have joined forces to call attention to the fact that people of color in urban and rural communities and on tribal lands are far more likely to be "dumped on" than are white people of European ancestry in middle-income or affluent communities. For example, the nation's largest toxic waste dump, frequently called the nation's toilet, is in Emelle, Alabama, a city of primarily black residents, many of whom are middle class.

Two million tons of nuclear waste—radioactive uranium from mining operations—have contaminated tribal lands, and many health experts believe the toxic waste has contributed to the high rate of sexual-organ cancer among Navajo teenagers, a rate that is seventeen times higher than the national average for this age group. In Los Angeles, the smog capital of the United States, inner-city people who are primarily people of color suffer higher incidences of respiratory problems than do people who live in white enclaves with less air pollution. At least eight million children, most of whom are poor and members of minority groups, have been poisoned by lead from peeling paint and lead pipes in substandard housing, and by lead released in emissions from incinerators and toxic waste dumps.[2]

DOCUMENTING THE "RACE THING"

Community activists charge that for decades manufacturing and waste disposal companies have deliberately placed their polluting facilities in areas where, until recent years, people have not been organized to demand protection. The victims of contaminants usually have been powerless, unable to fight large corporations or the government agencies that were set up to protect the health of citizens but instead seem to ensure the profits of major companies. In the words of Susana Almanza, a community leader in Austin, Texas: "We are the real endangered species in America, people of color. We're the ones who are dying with the cancer clusters and the birth defects because of the air we breathe."[3] Almanza's group, made up of mostly people of color, was able to force a polluting gasoline terminal in their residential area to close.

In the 1970s, Robert D. Bullard, a sociologist at the University of California at Riverside, began to scientifically document the factors that determine where dirty industries and waste disposal sites have been located. He compiled the data for his wife, an attorney, who later filed a lawsuit for a middle-class black community in suburban Houston, Texas, charging discrimination in the placement of municipal landfills.

During several years of research, Bullard found that of the five landfills operated by the city of Houston, which is predominantly white, all were located in black neighborhoods. Out of eight waste incinerators, six were in primarily black communities. One was in El Segundo Barrio, a Latino neighborhood. Only one small incinerator was in a white area, and it "was supposed to be pollution-free. But it was not pollution-free, and . . . those white folks got the incinerator closed, and in the process all the incinerators had to be closed," Bullard said during one of his many public lectures on the subject.[4]

Although the lawsuit against the city of Houston did

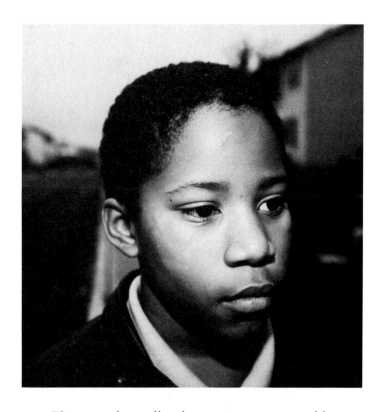

*This young boy suffers from eye irritation caused by
leakage from the landfill next to the projects where he lives.*

not succeed, Bullard with the support of a National Science
Foundation grant was prompted to investigate other southern cities. During the early 1980s, he uncovered an insidi-
ous "pattern of where hazardous waste landfills, hazardous
waste incinerators, municipal landfills, lead smelters, [and]
chemical plants" were located. He concluded, "It's not a
poverty thing. It's a race thing."

Communities most affected by polluting facilities were
those whose residents were primarily people of color—usually identified as African American, Native American, or

Asian, and sometimes of Spanish-speaking ancestry. However, whites of low-income status live in older urban or rural communities that have become dumping grounds, too. Affluent and middle-income people of color also were more apt to be victims of pollution than were whites of the same socioeconomic status. As Bullard explained, African-American communities have long been segregated from primarily white suburban or urban neighborhoods because of redlining—the now illegal practice of steering people of color to segregated neighborhoods for home sales—and other types of housing discrimination. Because the residents were nonwhite, their communities became targets for dumping. In short, segregation and institutional racism "influenced the siting of industrial facilities," he said.[5]

The link between race and pollution also was documented in a special study undertaken with the support of the United Church of Christ (UCC) Commission for Racial Justice. Staff member Charles Lee directed an eighteen-month survey to determine where the majority of the nation's 415 federally approved hazardous waste disposal sites were located. He then wrote a report titled *Toxic Waste and Race in the United States*, which was published in 1987 by the commission.

The survey and the UCC involvement in environmental issues came about primarily because of Benjamin F. Chavis, Jr., executive director of the National Association for the Advancement of Colored People. In 1982, Chavis responded to a request for help from a citizen group in Warren County, North Carolina. The group hoped to stop the state from dumping toxic waste in their community. Without informing residents of the area, who are predominantly of African American descent, the state planned to dump soil contaminated with cancer-causing polychlorinated biphenyls (PCBs) in a land site atop a groundwater source that sits close to the surface.

Warren County residents feared their drinking water would be contaminated with seeping chemicals. So Dollie

11

Burwell and her pastor, Leon White, organized demonstrators to try to block trucks loaded with six thousand tons of PCB-laced soil. The group, which swelled to five hundred in number, literally put their "lives on the line," Burwell said. "We did that by laying our bodies in front of the trucks, but as we lay there we knew that we were neither politically [nor] economically empowered enough to stop those trucks . . . . we were hauled off to jail by the busload."[6]

Although the Warren County demonstration did not stop the state from dumping PCBs, the action brought media attention and prompted the UCC study. The research showed that three out of every five people of color live near a hazardous waste site. The commission found that race was a "more prominent factor" than the economic status of the nearby residents in determining location of toxic waste sites, although poor whites also lived near these facilities.

Chavis called the practice of concentrating environmental hazards in minority communities "environmental racism." He further defined the term as "racial discrimination in environmental policymaking and the enforcement of regulations and laws, the deliberate targeting of people-of-color communities for toxic waste facilities, the official sanctioning of the life-threatening presence of poisons and pollutants in our communities, and the history of excluding people of color from leadership in the environmental movement."[7]

Still another report documenting the relationship between race and hazardous waste sites was issued by University of Michigan researchers who studied an area surrounding Detroit. Their report was presented at a January 1990 conference and was published later in the Proceedings of the Michigan Conference on Race and the Incidence of Environmental Hazards. According to data included in the study, people of color were four times more likely than whites to live near a hazardous waste facility, and race, not income, was a major factor in the proximity to the waste disposal site.[8]

OPPOSING VIEWS

After release of the 1987 UCC commission report, the U.S. Environmental Protection Agency (EPA), which licenses and regulates hazardous waste disposal facilities and approves site locations, refuted the findings. The agency said that the process of selecting locations for waste facilities was based on "strictly technical" data, such as whether the land was suitable for waste disposal and whether the site could be properly lined to prevent leaking of hazardous materials.[9]

Officials of waste disposal companies and industries known for polluting practices also deny that racist attitudes determine where their facilities have been or will be placed. According to one congressional report, those who deny or doubt that environmental racism exists say that "People reside in the vicinity of waste treatment facilities and other potential pollution sources . . . because they are attracted by employment opportunities, favorable prices for real estate, and the relatively high standard of living (compared to other affordable areas)."[10]

According to such a view, high disease rates in polluted communities are more likely due to lack of health care and to unhealthy lifestyles than to exposure to hazardous materials. Some believe that poor people and members of minority groups are inherently more susceptible to serious diseases than are members of the dominant middle class. They cited no evidence to support their contentions, however.

ENVIRONMENTAL JUSTICE ISSUES

Since the late 1980s, community groups led by people of color have used the term Chavis coined—"environmental racism"—to call attention to various dumping practices that adversely affect people of color and the poor more than middle-income whites. "Environmental justice" has been the rallying cry for a variety of grassroots and regional and

13

national organizations, which declare that no group in the United States, or in other parts of the world, should have to bear a disproportionate share of environmental pollution. Social justice demands that all people be protected.

In October 1991, the First National People of Color Environmental Leadership Summit convened in Washington, D.C., bringing together more than six hundred activists—people of color in leadership roles who represented community groups from every state in the union and from Puerto Rico, the Marshall Islands, Central America, and Canada. The conference, sponsored by the United Church of Christ Commission for Racial Justice, called attention to life-and-death environmental issues that people of color have to face. And because of this "dramatic display of environmental and social justice activism by people of color" at the summit, it was clear to many Americans from a wide range of backgrounds that "the environmental movement in the United States changed forever," according to Charles Lee, who coordinated the conference.

Lee pointed out in his introduction to the proceedings of the conference, published in 1992, that "many themes shaped the discussions of the Summit," not the least of which was the concept that "[we] people of color must speak for ourselves."[11]

Indeed, conference members defined the principles of environmental justice, which affirmed the interdependence of all species on earth and the sacredness of Mother Earth. Other principles are the fundamental right of all people to clean air, water, and land, and the right to political, economic, cultural, and environmental self-determination. Industries must stop producing poisonous materials, including hazardous waste and radioactive materials, and producers of toxins must be accountable for damage to the earth and its inhabitants.

This book focuses on a great variety of environmental problems that have adversely affected communities made up of people of color. These problems include hazardous materials in industrial workplaces such as steel mills, construction sites, garment factories, and semiconductor industries, where laborers are predominantly people of color.

Another problem is the long history of lead poisoning among children of low-income families, due in part to inadequate public health programs to protect people from lead hazards. Other environmental justice issues include the toxic threat to Native American lands and the overuse of pesticides that poison many migrant farmworkers who have little power to protest.

Finally, the link between poverty and pollution on a global scale is covered. And the last chapter looks at some of the actions of grassroots groups and national organizations that are trying to change the policies that allow industries to dump on the powerless.

2

EXPLOITING THE POWERLESS

Since the 1600s, when adventurers from the European nations explored and conquered lands in Africa, Asia, and the Americas, the powerless have experienced environmental pollution and the abuse of natural resources. For centuries Native Americans filled their basic needs through the sustainable use of natural resources. Tribal groups hunted, fished, planted crops, and gathered from the land in ways that did not deplete the environment, taking from nature only what they needed at the time. This way of living in harmony with the natural environment was reflected in laws of the Iroquois Confederacy, which stated: "In our every deliberation, we must consider the impact of our decisions on the next seven generations."

But the Native American way of life began to change in the late 1700s, after American colonists gained their independence from Britain. As pioneers began to push westward, they urged the U.S. government to buy Indian lands so as to open up more territory for settlers as well as for industries, roads, rail lines, and other human activities. The wars and treaties that followed were designed to force tribal groups from their lands. Native Americans were exiled to territories on which they could barely provide for their basic needs. This forced resettlement resulted in poverty, poor health, and social problems for many Indian nations.

During the 1800s, as the factory system grew in the United States, much of the rural population moved to cities, primarily in the East and Midwest and along the West Coast. Low prices for crops and heavy debt from farming forced many people to leave rural areas and to seek jobs in growing industries. Millions of immigrants from Europe also arrived, and most settled in cities—New York in particular, since it was the nation's largest seaport.

Many of the new arrivals were poor and had to live in city slums, areas that today would be labeled "blighted" or "deteriorated" or "low-income neighborhoods." People crowded into small shacks or low-rent tenements that were not much more than wooden barracks with no sanitary facilities and little ventilation. Because industries were nearby, these neighborhoods were also permeated with coal soot from factory smokestacks. Observers of the time often called these slums pigsties, although it could be argued that pigs on farms had healthier living conditions.

EARLY ENVIRONMENTALISTS

Since the early 1900s, local, state, and federal programs in the United States have attempted to address the problems of the urban poor. Programs have concentrated on preventing crime and drug abuse and providing community services such as improved housing, garbage collection, health aid, schooling, street repairs, and job training. Although some programs have been designed to clean up the physical surroundings in impoverished communities, most efforts have been aimed at social and public health problems. Seldom have these programs included an environmental effort. For that matter, even conservation efforts have a relatively short history.

For several hundred years the prevailing view in American society was that individuals should be allowed to conquer and exploit nature for short-term economic benefits. However, during the late 1800s and early 1900s, a few conservationists—those who believed in using natural resources wisely—began to speak out and organize. John Muir was an example.

An early American conservationist, Muir established the Sierra Club in 1892 to protect the natural habitats of the Sierra Nevada range in the western United States. The club expanded over the years to become one of the largest environmental groups in the nation. Other groups formed, too, such as the American Forestry Association, the National Wildlife Federation, the National Audubon Society, and the Wilderness Society. But since the inception of the major conservation and environmental groups—even those formed from the 1960s through the 1980s—members and leaders have been primarily affluent white people. Few people of color have been part of mainstream environmental organizations, although there are programs under way now to change that situation.

One reason for the lack of diversity stems from the racist attitudes and the prejudice that have been part of American culture. Most environmental organizations deliberately excluded nonwhites and non-Christians—Jews, for example. In many cases immigrants from southern and eastern Europe, many of whom were Catholics, also were barred from membership, because early conservationists believed these new arrivals would continue European hunting practices that destroyed wildlife.[1]

CIVIL RIGHTS VERSUS ENVIRONMENTALISM

When the civil rights movement was in full swing during the 1960s and 1970s, the modern environmental movement also sprouted, focusing much public attention on America's filthy waterways, polluted air, and littered landscapes. Although the civil rights and environmental movements had many common interests and concerns—protecting public

18

health was one of them—their agendas seldom merged. In fact they were often in conflict. For example, most environmentalists seemed to give top priority to saving natural habitats and wildlife for recreational use and to preserving the beauty of nature. But people of color had long been barred by local laws or customs from many public parks, beaches, and other natural areas, so they hardly were inclined to join in conservation programs.

Another conflict stemmed from the fact that civil rights groups were concerned with achieving basic constitutional rights and overturning discriminatory laws and practices. Many people of color and the poor also had to worry about survival—finding and keeping jobs to provide income for basic needs. The upper-middle-class members of environmental groups, of course, seldom faced such problems; few knew how the poor lived or what obstacles people of color encountered in their daily lives. Some civil rights activists have observed that most environmentalists could empathize more with dolphins and trees than with people dying of diseases linked to industrial toxins.

Mistrust has been another factor contributing to the fissure between environmentalists and civil rights activists. Some people of color, especially those who were deeply involved in the civil rights struggle of the past decades, suspect that environmentalists want to divert public attention and funding away from equal justice issues.

American industry and politicians, touting the benefits of economic development, also have played a part in creating divisions between environmental and civil rights groups. Frequently companies guilty of causing pollution have fought environmental regulations by claiming that jobs would be lost if the industries had to meet environmental standards. Because low-income people, whatever their ethnic background, would be most hurt by the job losses, company representatives and politicians could easily convince workers that environmentalists were to blame for factory layoffs and even for plant closings. In addition, some believe that companies have made generous contributions to civil rights groups to silence protests over unhealthy working conditions and environmental pollution.

Since the 1980s, however, hundreds of grassroots groups have organized across the United States to fight environmental degradation in their communities. Many are led by people of color and others who have never before taken an activist role. Whatever their cultural or economic background, most groups are not well known except in their local areas, but they have been working to make environmental justice a reality. In spite of powerful opposition, these groups have gained political power and have forced polluters to clean up or to stay out of their communities.

Today, because of efforts by people of color who are activists in their communities, major environmental organizations have become aware that they must help bridge the gaps between themselves and communities of color. There is still a long way to go, but some organizations, like the Sierra Club, the National Resources Defense Council, the Environmental Defense Fund, and Friends of the Earth, have established environmental justice programs that include efforts to recruit people of color for their staffs and boards.

Others have encouraged new chapters to organize in previously ignored urban areas. National Audubon Society president Peter Berle has been campaigning since 1984 to change the focus of his organization from a primary concern for birds and other wildlife to one that includes urban issues such as cleaning up polluted neighborhoods. Because of the society's change in approach, Emilio Williams, director of programs for the National Association of Service and Conservation Corps, got involved. Williams, of African American ancestry, told a *Washington Post* reporter: "We've been led to believe that environmental issues are not for black folks, but that's the biggest lie."[2] He now heads an Audubon chapter that was formed in 1992 in the Washington, D.C. area.

National environmental organizations also have created ties with various grassroots groups. These two movements can form politically powerful coalitions if both camps are able to work together. Activists in these coalitions hope to combat politicians and industrialists who for personal gain continue to target poor and powerless communities as sites for dirty industries and waste disposal.

TARGETING THE VULNERABLE

Some government officials and business leaders argue that poor communities welcome almost any kind of economic development no matter what the health risks. Indeed, many unemployed people who desperately need jobs point out that poverty is as hazardous to health as pollutants from a dirty factory, sewage plant, waste disposal site, highway, or airport. So they accept facilities in their midst that endanger their health and the health of their families and neighbors. In fact, when facilities that are potential polluters are proposed for some poor communities, civic leaders may hail them as a godsend, even shrugging off possible dangers as something people have to live with.

Sociologist Robert Bullard has described this situation as "environmental job blackmail." He explains that workers of color are especially vulnerable to job blackmail because they face a greater threat of unemployment than whites do and because of their concentration in low-paying, unskilled, nonunionized occupations. For example, they make up a large share of the nonunion contract workers in the oil, chemical, and nuclear industries, and are more easily fired and replaced than the union workers.

Similarly, over 95 percent of migrant farmworkers in the United States are Latino, African American, Afro-Caribbean, or Asian. And African Americans are overrepresented in high-risk, blue-collar and service occupations for which a large pool of replacement labor exists. Fear of unemployment acts as a potent incentive for many African American workers to accept and keep jobs they know are health threatening.[3]

Industries also target some groups for potentially hazardous jobs because the groups are stereotyped as submissive. The electronics industry in California, for example, seeks

21

This woman is an electonics assembler at
Hughes Aircraft in Burbank, California.
The electronics industry in California often
hires Asian women for assembly work,
believing that these workers will accept jobs
that expose them to highly toxic chemicals.

Asian women—primarily immigrants from China, Hong Kong, Korea, and Vietnam—for assembly work, believing that such workers will not make waves and, regardless of the health hazards, will accept jobs that involve exposure to highly toxic chemicals. A similar situation exists in the garment industry on both the West Coast and the East Coast. Because they need the income, many women of color work in manufacturing plants that some say are as bad as the sweatshops (unhealthy factories where people toiled for long hours at low pay) of the early 1900s.

When new factories or waste disposal facilities are planned, company owners or managers and government officials continue to try to locate—and often succeed in placing—unsightly or contaminating operations in vulnerable communities. In New York, for example, the state's largest incinerator for medical waste was originally planned for a suburban area in Rockland County. But instead it was placed in the South Bronx, a densely populated low-income neighborhood. In addition, New York City officials plan to build seven more incinerators in low-income neighborhoods where residents are likely to be exposed to "7,000 tons of poisonous gas [emissions] a year," according to a report in the *New York Times*.[4]

In Georgia there have been numerous attempts to locate waste disposal sites and polluting industries in poor rural areas, many of which are predominantly black communities, prompting charges of environmental racism. One plan was to locate a 900-acre landfill in Hancock County, Georgia, where the majority of residents are of African American ancestry. In February 1993, the Georgia Supreme Court refused to grant a permit for that installation, which would have accepted trash not only from across the state but also from states as far away as New Jersey.

Nevertheless, other proposals for placing potentially hazardous facilities are still under consideration. They include plans to build a large medical waste incinerator, a $40 million lead battery recycling plant, a burner for carpet scrap, and a sewage treatment plant. Again, proposed sites for these facilities are areas where people traditionally have not resisted political decisions. The medical waste incinerator, for example, is planned for Quitman County, which is about equally divided between black residents and whites, but would be in an area that comprises primarily people of color. In fact the incinerator would be built near a black church, the Hopewell Missionary Baptist Church. Mattie Lee, who teaches Sunday school there, said that the site selection was based on racist attitudes. "You think they'd do this to a white church?" she asked a reporter.[5]

In Burke County, many residents also are convinced their community has been targeted. According to one community activist, Barbara Cunningham, "Nearly everyone on Quaker Road [where the battery plant would be located] is black. This says to me that they're trying to put it in a minority neighborhood."[6]

U.S. Representative Cynthia McKinney of Georgia, who has studied the problems of waste disposal in her state, came to a similar conclusion. In her view, "It is certainly evident that the poor, minority, and rural areas of the South have actually borne the brunt of the lack of any kind of cohesive waste management policy on the national, state, and local levels."[7]

Along with Georgia, the southern states of Louisiana, Mississippi, Alabama, South Carolina, Arkansas, and Texas have become dumping grounds for hazardous waste. South Carolina, for example, has the nation's largest toxic waste site, and Alabama harbors the largest radioactive waste disposal facility.

Large corporations frequently have been lured to the South by generous tax breaks—that is, government officials make companies exempt from paying property taxes or other taxes if they set up operations in their state and promise jobs. Author Donald Schueler reported in late 1992 that his home state, Louisiana, provided "$2.5 billion in property-tax exemptions during the 1980s" to thirty large corporations, even though they "created few permanent jobs."

Many of the corporations were known to be "the country's worst polluters."[8]

Schueler explained that one reason for such arrangements is that many southern towns are "company towns"—that is, one or two large industries are the only source of income for a specific community, and those industries are then able to intimidate workers, threatening to fire employees who complain about dangerous working conditions or environmental pollution. People who publicly oppose companies that pollute may also be subject to harassment by neighbors and co-workers who fear for their livelihood or who do not believe that pollution is a problem.

A RACIAL IMBALANCE IN CLEANUP OPERATIONS

Compounding the problem in the South and elsewhere in the nation is the fact that once polluting facilities become part of a community, law enforcement may be lax in regard to cleanup operations. This is a particular problem in areas where people of color make up the majority of the population. After a major investigation in 1992, the *National Law Journal* (*NLJ*) reported that "The federal government, in its cleanup of hazardous sites and its pursuit of polluters, favors white communities over minority communities under environmental laws meant to provide equal protection for all citizens."[9]

Using EPA data and reports available to the public, the *NLJ* analyzed enforcement of environmental regulations under the Resource Conservation and Recovery Act (RCRA) of 1976 (amended in 1984 to address disposal of hazardous and solid wastes) and the Comprehensive Environmental Response, Compensation and Liability Act of 1980. The 1980 legislation set up a fund, now known as Superfund, to clean up hazardous waste sites. But according to *NLJ* findings, there has been a racial imbalance in law enforcement under RCRA and Superfund.

Regardless of income level, penalties were 46 percent

higher for violations in predominantly white communities than for the same type of violations in nonwhite areas. According to the report, the average fine for polluting industries was $355,566 for mostly white areas and $53,318 for areas populated primarily by people of color. Thus, to avoid stiff fines, companies in white areas are likely to try not to violate environmental laws. In addition, "Under the giant Superfund cleanup program, abandoned hazardous waste sites in minority areas take 20 percent longer to be placed on the national priority action list than those in white areas," the NLJ reported.[10]

Among the examples cited was West Dallas, Texas, a Latino and black community located near a lead smelter that for decades had contaminated the area with high levels of lead, an extremely poisonous metal. When ingested, lead can cause brain damage, kidney disease, blindness, and other serious disabilities. The state shut down the smelter in 1984 only after a lengthy lawsuit, which was filed in 1981 on behalf of 370 children who lived in the area and suffered lead poisoning. (The children were finally awarded $20 million in damages in 1985.)

Cleanup operations took place and supposedly were completed in 1985. But the Centers for Disease Control (CDC), a federal agency designed to protect public health, found that children living in the area had lead levels twice as high as the level considered safe at that time—about 25 micrograms of lead per deciliter of blood. The level that CDC now considers safe has dropped to 10 micrograms per deciliter, discussed in more detail in the next chapter. Many children as well as adults suffer health problems that include constant nosebleeds, bleeding gums, arthritic pains, and impaired mental capabilities.

A coalition of multiracial and multicultural grassroots groups struggled for years to get the EPA and state and city officials to admit that further cleanup was necessary. Finally, in 1992, the EPA began removing lead-contaminated soil from areas that the agency previously had labeled "clean."[11]

Another problem area described was a Latino community in Tucson, Arizona, near a Hughes aircraft plant that builds planes for the air force. For at least three decades the plant dumped trichloroethylene (TCE), a solvent used in cleaning products such as degreasers, into pits on the base. The National Cancer Institute has linked TCE to cancer of the liver, and the solvent may cause a number of other serious diseases. TCE seeped through the soil to an aquifer—a source of drinking water for 47,000 people—and concentration levels exceeded 300 parts per billion (ppb). The EPA has set safety levels at no more than 5 ppb.

Government officials discovered the TCE contamination in 1981 and shut down the wells. Two years later the site was placed on the Superfund list. But the plume of contaminated water continued to move underground, forcing the shutdown of other drinking wells. To date, little has been done to clean up the water supply, and federal agencies such as the EPA and the U.S. Department of Health and Human Services claim that there is no evidence directly linking TCE to adverse health effects. But in the Tucson community along Calle Evelina, known as the "Street of Death," residents in twenty-seven out of thirty houses had died of cancer as of fall 1992.[12]

People living with these health problems have felt hopeless and helpless. Many have expressed doubt that state or federal government agencies will ever do anything to clean up their contaminated communities, although some action may be taken as a result of recent activism by grassroots groups.

ENVIRONMENTAL EQUITY

Since the late 1980s, an increasing number of people of color—grassroots activists, religious leaders, scholars in the social sciences and the environment—have publicly questioned whether state and federal EPA agencies have discharged their duties fairly, protecting all citizens from environmental pollution. In 1990, William Reilly, who was then EPA administrator, asked a task force of thirty members to study the issue. Two years later, the agency released its findings in a 49-page report titled "Environmental Equity: Reducing Risks for All Communities."

The report concluded that people of color experience a "greater than average" exposure to environmental pollutants, including lead, carbon monoxide, sulfur dioxide, emissions from hazardous waste dumps, and contaminated fish from polluted waterways. But the task force blamed this disparity on housing patterns, land ownership and use, and lack of political power. Robert Wolcott, an EPA official who led the task force, said "It comes down to resources to place oneself in jobs and homes that avoid exposure. In many cases, racial minorities don't have the capital. . . ."[13]

Yet crucial questions remained: If escape was not possible, why were industries continuing to dump their pollutants in communities where people were trapped? Why did industries continue to try to place new potentially hazardous facilities in communities that had little power to fight back? Why did government officials continue to allow such actions? In the minds of activists, this was discrimination—environmental racism—plain and simple.

This view was strengthened when an EPA official, Lewis Crampton, wrote a confidential memorandum detailing how the "politically explosive environmental issues" covered in the 1992 EPA report should be handled. The memo, which was leaked to the press, suggested that the EPA should plan to win over mainstream civil rights, religious, and union groups before grassroots activists could press their case. U.S. Representative Henry A. Waxman of California obtained a copy of the memo and released it at a congressional hearing, declaring that Crampton's plan was "a cynical divide-and-conquer strategy" that sought to "drive a wedge between activist groups and traditional civil rights organizations."[14]

Longtime civil rights activist Benjamin Chavis called the plan for publicizing the EPA report "pretty pathetic."

In his view, the EPA ought to "engage in dialogue with the [civil rights] community on some of its critical issues" rather than attempt to "seduce members of the community."[15]

Over the following year, however, changes began to take place at the federal level. After President Bill Clinton took office, his administration announced that environmental justice would be a top priority. Carol Browner, administrator of the EPA, has repeatedly declared that the concept of environmental equity should be dealt with on a daily basis, not in a piecemeal fashion as had been true in the past. She also has taken steps to attack injustices through stricter enforcement of environmental laws and regulations. In mid-1993, the EPA announced that it would begin a study of several hundred communities around Superfund sites—those known to be the most hazardous waste sites in the nation—that are located in communities made up primarily of people of color.

Other members of Clinton's administration—Vice President Al Gore in particular—have attempted to educate the general public on the environmental justice issue. Gore has long argued for sweeping policy changes in the United States and other nations in order to protect the earth and its inhabitants, and he has urged citizens and politicians to work together on this effort. People "must be politically empowered to demand and help effect remedies to ecological problems . . . wherever people at the grassroots level are deprived of a voice in the decisions that affect their lives, they and the environment suffer," Gore wrote in his book *Earth in the Balance,* published in 1992. He has repeated that theme in numerous speeches since, as he did in his address to the Black Church Environmental Justice Summit held in Washington, D.C., in December 1993. During that occasion, Gore praised ministers and other private citizens in communities of color who have led the way in the fight against environmental racism, noting that "It is time for this nation to respond to this crisis . . . and we are beginning to respond."

In February 1994, President Bill Clinton issued an exec-

NAACP executive director the Reverend Benjamin Chavis (left), and Vice President Albert Gore exchange views at the Summit on Environmental Justice in Washington, D.C., December 3, 1993. The Vice President announced that the Clinton administration would respond to the "crisis of disproportionate pollution in minority communities."

utive order that basically requires each federal agency to make environmental justice part of its mission. With his order, the president also mandated the creation of an Interagency Working Group that will develop strategies to achieve environmental justice.

3
LEAD POISONING VICTIMS

After years of neglect, pollution-related health problems caused by racial and class inequities may finally be addressed as the EPA and other federal agencies and departments change course. But in the past, the federal government has pointed out imbalances in population exposure to toxic lead. These imbalances were described in a 1988 report by the Agency for Toxic Substances and Disease Registry, which is part of the U.S. Department of Health and Human Services.

In a brief analysis of the report, Janet Phoenix, a physician working in a lead-poisoning prevention program in Washington, D.C., noted that the Disease Registry study shows that "lead exposure is not randomly distributed across population groups. Its distribution is directly related to both class and race. A disproportionate impact, for example, is felt in African American communities, as are so many environmental health problems. . . . Indeed, African Americans, at all class levels, have a significantly greater chance of being lead poisoned than do whites."[1]

31

WHAT IS LEAD POISONING?

Lead serves no purpose in the human body, but once ingested, it may stay in the body unless one undergoes treatment to remove it. After entering the body, lead circulates in the bloodstream for a few weeks and then is absorbed into the bone, just as calcium would be (the body mistakes lead for calcium because it has no way of differentiating between the two metallic elements). Because they are still developing, young children absorb about 50 percent of the lead to which they are exposed, while adults absorb only about 10 percent.

Up until about the 1970s, medical experts thought lead poisoning occurred when the level of lead in the blood was 50 to 60 micrograms per deciliter (microg/dl) of blood. Then a person exhibited problems with the nerves in arms and legs and abdominal pain and stomach cramps. But studies since the 1970s have shown that much lower levels of lead in the blood have an adverse effect. Consequently, the lead level considered dangerous has been dropping steadily over the past two decades. By 1985 the Centers for Disease Control had defined lead poisoning as a blood level of 25 microg/dl.

Researchers continued studying the effects of lead exposure, particularly in children. Studies compared children with low levels of lead—for example, 4 or 5 microg/dl—with those whose levels were above 25 microg/dl. It was found that even though physical symptoms might not be apparent, lead in the body affected children's behavior and intelligence. In late 1991, the Centers for Disease Control released guidelines that again redefined the nature and scope of lead exposure and poisoning, and set a standard for lead poisoning at 10 microg/dl.

THOSE MOST AT RISK

Fetuses, infants, and young children are at the greatest risk of poisoning from lead. Pregnant women exposed to lead can transmit the toxin to their fetuses, which may cause premature birth and low birth weight in infants. During early childhood, a youngster who ingests just a milligram daily of lead-paint dust, which is equivalent to a few granules of sugar, can become severely poisoned.

According to Suzanne Binder, medical director of the Lead Poisoning Prevention Branch at the Centers for Disease Control, lead-poisoned children "have lower IQs, develop more slowly, do not reach their developmental milestones in infancy, have behavioral disturbances that will be noted by teachers, and have other biochemical abnormalities that wouldn't be picked up during a routine physical examination."[2]

Children with high levels of lead may suffer brain damage, blindness, kidney problems, and other serious disabilities. In some cases of severe lead poisoning, permanent damage may be prevented or diminished with chelation, a medical procedure using injections to cleanse the blood of lead.

Youngsters may absorb lead from dust in the air and by touching surfaces coated with lead-based paint, such as windowsills, and then putting their fingers in their mouths. Young children may also eat flakes of lead paint, which taste sweet, rather like lemon drops. Playing in areas where the soil contains lead is one more way children ingest the toxic metal. Lead-contaminated drinking water also contributes to accumulation of lead, and possible poisoning, in youngsters.

An estimated three million American children have lead levels of 10 microg/dl. Lead poisoning, in fact, is considered the most serious environmental threat faced by children across the United States. But the risk appears to be the greatest in inner cities.

In 1993, a team of medical researchers in the Washington, D.C., area reported the results of blood tests of 4,500 children living in urban, suburban, and rural areas. The children tested ranged in age from nine months to three years. Of the 4,200 urban children tested, 780 children (19

This incinerator is located at a low-income housing project in New York City. Poisonous gases come from incinerator smoke and children are especially at risk from flaking, lead-based paint found in older apartments. The rates of lead poisoning are very high among inner-city children.

percent) had blood-lead concentrations above 10 microg/dl, while seventy-one children tested higher than 25 microg/dl. By contrast, among the 212 suburban youngsters tested, only five children tested at 10 microg/dl, and seven of the 120 rural children tested were at that level. None of the suburban or rural participants had lead levels above 15 microg/dl.[3]

Some workers, such as those on construction jobs, also are at high risk of lead poisoning. Although the U.S. Occupational Safety and Health Administration established regulations in 1978 to protect many industrial workers from lead hazards, the rules did not apply to the construction industry until mid-1993. As a result, people such as ironworkers, utility line workers, and those tearing down or repairing bridges and other structures have been exposed for years to daily doses of lead-laden dust and fumes. They have even carried lead particles home in their clothing and on their skin and hair, thus exposing their families to the toxic metal.

Among construction workers, long-term exposure to lead has caused abdominal problems, hypertension (high blood pressure), stroke, kidney disease, and nerve damage. Those who suffer poisoning may have flulike symptoms such as achy joints, nausea, and fatigue.

MAJOR SOURCES OF TOXIC LEAD

Today Americans probably consume one hundred times more lead than prehistoric humans did, and numerous scientific studies on lead poisoning prompted the U.S. Congress to ban the addition of lead to gasoline. (Lead was used as an additive in gasoline to reduce engine knocking.) But even though the Clean Air Act of 1970 outlawed lead additives in gasoline and these have been nearly phased out, the air, soil, and waterways near highways, industries, and waste disposal sites can be contaminated with lead.

Lead-based paint and lead in dust and soil are the major sources of lead in the environment today, in spite of a 1977 ban on the manufacture of lead paint. The lead content of paint in older homes may be as high as 30 parts per hundred, or 30 percent lead. Federal agencies such as the Centers for Disease Control and the Department of Housing and Urban Development estimate that 57 million American homes contain lead. Three-fourths of all housing built before 1980 contain lead paint on walls, windowsills, doorframes, cupboards, and other surfaces.[4]

Lead from smelters and other industries also contaminates soil and covers nearby surfaces as described in the case of West Dallas. Residents of many urban communities in the United States have had to live with this problem, as have millions of workers in such industries as construction and auto and battery manufacturing, who have been exposed to high levels of lead.

LEAD IN WATER SUPPLIES

Some water supplies also are contaminated with lead. Water sources such as reservoirs, lakes, streams, and underground aquifers, are usually free of lead, but as water travels from wells through mains and plumbing systems, it may dissolve lead from old lead pipes, lead-based solder, and faucets made with lead components. A 1986 federal law banned the use of lead in new plumbing systems, but many older municipal water systems and older buildings have plumbing systems that contain lead.

In May 1993 the EPA reported that 20 percent of the lead Americans ingest comes from drinking water. Out of 7,500 large and medium-sized water systems in the nation, 819 had lead levels higher than the safety standard of 15 parts per billion, the EPA reported.

Consumer Reports, which publishes findings on tests of many types of consumer products, also investigated lead in water supplies and found "clear lead hazards" in Chicago and Boston and "reason for concern" in San Francisco, New York, and Washington, D.C. The magazine noted that "Although Chicago sent the EPA data that indicated an almost lead-free water supply, our Chicago participants had a lead problem of major proportions. . . . Had Chicago reported lead levels like those we found, the EPA would have required the city's water utility to develop a public-information campaign, study and institute special lead-controlling water treatments, and perhaps eventually replace lead service lines and connections—the agency's standard remedies for cities that fail the first-round EPA test." Because of the discrepancies, the EPA began an investigation of Chicago's water-testing methods.[5]

THE SLOW PACE OF LEAD-ABATEMENT PROGRAMS

Because of the pervasiveness of lead in the environment, people at all social and economic levels can face health hazards posed by this toxic metal. But eliminating those hazards is easier for those who can pay for protective measures than for those who cannot afford safeguards. Even though lead hazards have been well documented and methods to prevent lead poisoning have been publicized for decades, public (government-funded) programs to prevent lead poisoning, particularly in nonwhite and poor communities, have been in short supply.

In 1952, for example, public health authorities in Baltimore, Maryland, reported that after twenty years of testing, the rate of childhood lead poisoning was 7.5 times higher among the black population than among the white population. In 1969 another report from researchers at the New Jersey College of Medicine stated that each year an estimated 200,000 children, primarily black and Puerto Rican, were added to the thousands already poisoned by lead, but little had been done in major U.S. cities to solve the problem.[6]

During the 1970s, several reports in the *Washington Post* called attention to the fact that the percentage of nonwhite children being poisoned by lead, usually from lead-based paint, was much greater than the percentage of white children. According to estimates at that time, at least 400,000 children each year were lead poisoned. In a 1973 editorial the *Post* stated the case clearly: "One reason the nation has never mounted a public health campaign against lead paint

37

poisoning is that it affects mostly the poor, the black, the Spanish speaking and others who often must endure miserable housing."[7]

The problem of lead poisoning received very little attention from federal officials during the 1980s. Funds were cut for lead-testing programs, cleanup of lead-contaminated housing, and medical treatment of children poisoned by lead. These funding cuts were made in spite of the fact that one study showed that an investment of $32 billion in cleanup of dilapidated housing could have saved more than $60 billion in costs for treating poisoned children.[8]

During the early 1990s, members of Congress proposed legislation to combat lead poisoning. But the bills became embroiled in controversy. One of the reasons for the conflict was a provision that called for home sellers to inform potential buyers of any lead paint in a home before purchase. According to a report in the New York Times, the National Association of Realtors conducted an intense lobbying campaign to have the provision deleted. The realtors said that the price of homes would rise $5,000 to $10,000 if homeowners were forced to eliminate lead hazards before selling their property. Home sales were already down because of poor economic conditions in the nation, and the realtors feared sales would drop further if prices increased.[9]

The provision, however, became part of regulations that were included in 1992 laws reauthorizing funds for federal housing programs. Taking effect in 1995, the notification provision also applies to rental property.

Other provisions of the legislation that became effective in 1992 authorized funds for programs to eliminate lead poisoning by the year 2012. The Centers for Disease Control will provide grants to clinics and other health facilities for such purposes. In addition, funds were provided to the EPA and the National Safety Council to launch a major educational campaign to prevent lead poisoning. The public education effort includes an information clearinghouse that can be reached through an 800 number (800-LEADFYI, or

800-532-3394), which provides explanations in English or Spanish about the hazards of lead and how to prevent poisoning or find treatment. Many state health departments also have set up special information services to help prevent lead poisoning. Some public health facilities also are providing low-cost or free blood tests to determine lead levels.

QUESTIONS ABOUT LEAD CLEANUP METHODS

One other provision of the 1992 lead-abatement legislation is a $375 million fund for a cleanup program in public housing. But billions of dollars will be needed to eliminate or reduce lead contamination in low-income communities. State and local governments, which must find income for many services, are not certain which strategies are the most cost-effective in removing lead. Some argue, for example, that money allocated to reduce lead in urban water supplies should be spent instead on rehabilitation of run-down housing, where lead levels are usually high.

Mary Ellen Mortensen, medical director of the lead clinic at Children's Hospital in Columbus, Ohio, pointed out that "By itself, the amount of lead in drinking water, even at [EPA's allowable 15 ppb] . . . is not going to produce high blood levels [of lead]." Dr. Mortensen was more concerned about poor housing with high levels of lead-based paint. Just one gram of lead-based paint—equivalent to the amount of lead on a polished fingernail—contains 500 to 1,000 times more lead than four liters of water with 15 ppb lead, she explained.[10]

Experts also disagree on the effectiveness of removing lead-laced soil from the yards of homes in contaminated industrial areas. A study published in the *Journal of the American Medical Association* in April 1993 found that "lead-contaminated soil contributes to the lead burden of urban children," but removing that soil from around homes resulted in only "a modest decline in blood lead levels."

Thus the researchers argued that soil removal, which cost about $9,600 per household, was not an effective means of lead abatement. Many other factors, such as loose lead paint in the home, contributed to high levels of lead in the blood of children tested. In the opinion of the researchers, the majority of urban children in the United States would not benefit greatly from removal of lead-contaminated soil near their homes. [11]

Meanwhile, as health experts and government officials try to find affordable ways to reduce lead hazards, low-income residents have few choices. Besides being unable to pay for protective measures in their homes, most do not have the money needed to move out of lead-contaminated areas. About all such residents can do is worry about their health while they continue to be exposed to lead, along with other toxic materials that frequently pollute such areas.

4

FIGHTING HAZARDOUS WASTE SITES AND TOXIC EMISSIONS

"Chemicals Taint Groundwater in Every State"
"The Poisoning of America: Hazardous Chemical
Wastes"
"Ravaged Communities Left with Toxic Legacy"
"Birth Defects: Living near Toxic Sites"
"Incinerator Health, Safety Issues Fuel Heated Debate"

These are just a few of the newspaper headlines that have called attention to hazardous waste dumping and toxic emissions since the late 1970s and early 1980s.

In addition dozens of studies on toxic chemicals and their effects have been published in scientific journals such as the *American Journal of Industrial Medicine,* the *American Journal of Epidemiology, Environmental Research,* and the *Journal of Occupational Medicine.* These studies clearly conclude that hazardous materials in solid waste and smokestack emissions from industry cause serious diseases such as cancer, respiratory problems, and birth defects.

WHAT ARE HAZARDOUS WASTES
AND EMISSIONS?

Toxic waste materials include gaseous emissions into the air as well as poisons in leftover products from manufacturing, processing, and other industrial activities, which end up in landfills and waterways. The largest quantities of hazardous waste that could cause death or illness come from oil refineries and chemical manufacturers, which generate at least half of the total toxic waste produced annually in the United States. Other manufacturing industries, agricultural industries, medical facilities, and research laboratories also produce large quantities of hazardous waste.

The 1976 U.S. Resource Conservation and Recovery Act (RCRA) defined hazardous waste as "waste which, because of its quantity, concentration, or physical, chemical, or infectious characteristics may (1) cause or contribute to an increase in mortality, or (2) pose a hazard to human health or the environment when improperly treated, stored, transported, disposed of, or otherwise managed." An increasing number of waste materials have been labeled hazardous since the law was passed, and provisions of the act regulate at least 250 million tons of hazardous waste each year.

Among the toxic materials in waste are metals such as arsenic, cadmium, copper, mercury, lead, and zinc, which occur naturally in the environment but are toxic when ingested in even small quantities. Toxic waste also includes many chlorinated hydrocarbons (compounds derived from petroleum products combined with chlorine) that do not usually occur in nature and tend to be poisonous. These compounds remain in the environment and become part of the food chain, with concentrations generally the highest in large birds, fish, and mammals.

The RCRA regulations prohibit the disposal of hazardous waste in landfills unless materials have been biologically or chemically treated to remove toxins. Then disposal is allowed only at sites where soil structure and special linings prevent leakage of toxins into the ground and into underground water sources.

No one knows how many of the 60,000 chemical compounds produced in the United States can actually harm people, since only a few have been studied extensively and regulated. Among those tested is dioxin, which is actually a group of chemical compounds, considered by most independent scientists to be the most potent carcinogen (cancer-causing compound) known. In laboratory studies of animals, dioxin also has caused reproductive problems and changes in the immune system.

DIOXINS

Dioxin can be found in wastes from some paper mills; the compound forms when chlorine is used for bleaching purposes. Dioxin is also released from chemical plants, herbicide manufacturers, metal smelters, and waste incinerators.

Since the 1970s there have been concerted efforts to downplay the risks of dioxin exposure. Some government and chemical and paper industry scientists have been insisting in recent years that dioxin is not as dangerous as once determined, and the New York Times has played a lead role in reporting such opinions.

On September 26, 1992, for example, the Times reported on a four-day meeting of independent scientists who reviewed dioxin studies and the first draft of an EPA report on dioxin. According to the article, "An independent panel of scientists concluded . . . that dioxin was not a large-scale cancer threat except to people exposed to unusually high levels of the toxic compound in chemical factories and from accidents."[1]

A number of other urban newspapers across the country reprinted this conclusion or used it as a basis for editorials, leading readers to believe that dioxin was not a widespread

*This park in the small city of Times Beach,
Missouri, is contaminated with deadly dioxin.*

public health hazard. However, scientists and other reporters for nationally distributed publications at the conference
found just the opposite to be true.

The *Wall Street Journal*, for example, reported: "Data
reviewed by an independent scientific panel suggest that
the danger from dioxin may be broader and more serious
than previously thought."[2] Earlier, on February 20, 1992,
the *Journal* had published a front-page story showing how
the paper and chlorine industries had waged a two-year
campaign to "create a fresh spin on the dioxin debate,"
quoting studies conducted by consultants paid by the paper
industry.[3]

In March 1993, the *New York Times* ran a series of
articles that questioned the nation's environmental policies
and once again included statements suggesting that dioxin
is not a major health threat.[4] These articles were reprinted
in a special issue of *Chemecology* magazine (May 1993), a
publication of the Chemical Manufacturers Association
that is circulated free to teachers and many other individuals
who might spread the word that dioxin is not as dangerous
as it was once thought to be. But debate about dioxin is
likely to continue, since some scientists continue to warn
about the dangers of this compound.

PCBs

Polychlorinated biphenyls (PCBs), mentioned in chapter 1,
are another group of chemical compounds that studies show
are health hazards. PCBs do not break down in water and do
not burn or conduct electricity. So companies such as General
Electric, Westinghouse, and Monsanto used PCBs for insulation in electrical appliances and in hydraulic fluid. Recent
court cases have shown that, as long ago as the 1930s, these
and other companies knew about skin diseases and other
health dangers that PCBs posed to employees working with
the chemicals, but did not make the information public. By
the mid-1960s, researchers in Sweden and other parts of
the world had documented the dangers of PCBs and the

Ella Moore, a resident of a Detroit neighborhood, watches as technicians fence off her property from the alley where concentrations of PCB were found. Nine homes adjoin the contaminated alley.

U.S. government finally banned the chemicals in 1976.

Nevertheless, large quantities of the compounds are still in the environment—in landfills, in the sediment of streams and lakes, and in oceans. PCBs concentrate in fatty tissue and accumulate in the food chain. Humans are exposed to these toxic chemicals through the food they eat, especially fish. The compounds not only cause cancer but are linked to reproductive problems and birth defects. Two studies published in 1990—one in *Neurotoxicology and Teratology* and the other in the *Journal of Pediatrics*—showed that infants with higher than average levels of PCB exposure were likely to suffer impaired motor skills and learning abilities.

BEGINNINGS OF GRASSROOTS ACTIVISM

Before scientific studies and federal and state laws began to widely address the effects of hazardous materials in the environment, many industries legally emitted toxins into the air and dumped manufacturing waste directly into waterways or into landfills, ditches, and similar sites. Some of these dumps, which total more than 1,200 nationwide, were eventually designated for cleanup under the Superfund law.

One such site was an abandoned two-mile-long trench in Niagara Falls, New York, called Love Canal, an area that has come to symbolize toxic dumping. Love Canal was originally planned for barge traffic from the upper to the lower Niagara River, but the canal was never completed. Instead, from 1942 to 1953, the deep trench became a disposal site for nearly 21,000 tons of toxic waste from industries. When the two-mile-long gully was filled up, the local government bought the land, covered the toxic materials with dirt, then built a school on the site.

A little more than twenty years later, the place began to take on the appearance of a Hollywood set for a horror film. Toxic muck oozed out of the earth and into basements. Giant cavities appeared in the ground. Trees and plants died. Chemical residues from pesticide manufacturing bubbled up in the school playground. Residents in the area reported health problems that included skin rashes, blood disorders, breathing difficulties, and birth defects.

After watching her children develop multiple health problems, one resident, Lois Gibbs, took action. She polled her neighbors to find out if they were suffering any unusual disorders. Mothers reported miscarriages, stillbirths, and babies with birth defects. Gibbs, who never before had considered community activism, let alone group leadership,

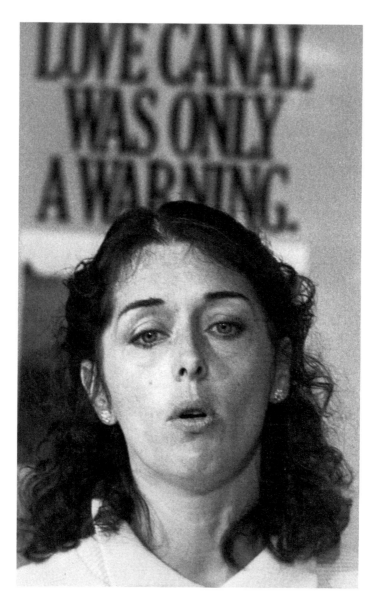

Lois Gibbs is the founder of the Love Canal
Homeowner's Association, one of the first grassroots
groups to defend their community against toxic
pollution endangering their homes and families.

organized one of the first grassroots efforts to fight against toxic waste sites in people's backyards. She became president of the Love Canal Homeowners Association, which included over nine hundred families. The group struggled from 1978 to 1980 to obtain public funds needed to move away from the contaminated neighborhood.

The initial information that Gibbs and her neighbors compiled helped prompt the state health department to study the situation. Then, in 1978, public health officials published a report with a title that spoke for itself: "Love Canal: Public Health Time Bomb." Eventually, under federal emergency orders, state officials evacuated families from the Love Canal area, buying and boarding up homes and the school.

Several other studies published during the 1980s in *Science, Human Biology,* and other scientific journals, showed that children who were born in Love Canal and lived most of their childhood there experienced slow growth and development and suffered adverse health effects from skin rashes to seizures linked to toxic chemicals in the environment. In 1991, the National Academy of Science published a review of the studies, finding them valid.

During and after the widely publicized evacuation of Love Canal, Gibbs and others in the original homeowners group received numerous calls from people across the United States. They wanted advice about toxic dumps in their neighborhoods. "What can we do?" they asked. "How can we get rid of toxins in our backyards?"

In 1981, to help answer those questions, the homeowners group became the Citizens' Clearinghouse for Hazardous Waste whose motto is "Helping People to Help Themselves." In the view of this organization, public policy should change from the bottom up. Instead of bringing in outside experts to tell people what to do, the clearinghouse provides resources—organizational training, information, and technical assistance—so that local groups can organize and speak for themselves.

Although not widely recognized until recent years, the

1970s and 1980s were a time when many people of color were also organizing to combat environmental injustices. At first, the rallying cry of local groups protesting toxic waste dumps or incinerators in their communities was "Not in My Backyard." But as groups became more aware of similar problems in other people's backyards, the protest broadened to "Not in Anyone's Backyard" or "No One's Backyard." Thousands of local groups now are part of a growing political force in the United States: the grassroots movement for environmental justice.

Some grassroots groups are made up of workers protesting toxic materials in the workplace. Other groups are affiliated with the Boston-based National Toxics Campaign, or with international environmental organizations such as Greenpeace and the Natural Resources Defense Council. These groups support programs to eliminate toxic hazards, whether from waste disposal sites or from manufacturing facilities that emit poisonous air pollutants.

Others are student groups that organize because of a local concern about hazardous pollutants. One example is a group of Latino teenagers in Brooklyn, New York, who organized in 1988 to inform their neighbors about the dangers of a toxic waste site in their community of Williamsburg. Calling themselves Toxic Avengers, the students have been campaigning to stop the construction of a hazardous waste incinerator nearby. Both the waste site and the incinerator proposed for their community are the result of environmental racism, according to the Toxic Avengers. One spokesperson claimed that waste management companies assume Latinos have no regard for their communities, but this community does care and wants the toxic waste site out.

BATTLES AGAINST HAZARDOUS
WASTE INCINERATORS

Along with regulating hazardous waste sites, the RCRA also sets standards for incinerators and some boilers and industrial furnaces that are allowed to burn hazardous waste, and it regulates cement kilns that burn hazardous waste for fuel. These facilities burn about five million tons of hazardous waste each year. Waste is burned at extremely high temperatures, from about 1,800°F to 2,500°F, and provisions of the law require that ash from burned materials or gas emitted through smokestacks must be free of 99.99 percent of the hazardous components before being released into the environment.

The EPA, which oversees hazardous waste burning, has long insisted that incinerators meeting RCRA standards are safe. In 1992, for example, Robert Holloway, EPA's expert on incineration who wrote some of the RCRA legislation, told a reporter: "The agency is confident its regulations will ensure the public health. It is a given that incinerators will emit toxic stuff, metals, acid gases. But . . . the question is, are the emissions at levels of acceptable risk? The agency is confident that the emissions do not pose an unacceptable risk."[5] Again in early 1993, Holloway reportedly said, "Properly designed incineration systems are proven and capable of achieving the highest overall degree of destruction and control."[6]

Opponents of hazardous waste incinerators, many of whom are members of multiracial grassroots organizations, argue that the technology is unproven, and they point to numerous problems such as fires and explosions at several facilities. There have been other problems as well. Since incinerators cannot destroy all of the hazardous waste, they generate toxic emissions, including gases that contain heavy metals and wastewater with toxic chemicals that are dumped into nearby streams.

In 1992, reporters for the *Pittsburgh Press* reviewed "hundreds of federal and state records" and conducted "dozens of interviews, many at the incinerators," which showed "that despite technological advances, the commercial hazardous waste industry . . . suffer[s] from accidents, violations of environmental rules, inconsistent government oversight and a negative public perception."[7]

51

Fighting toxic waste incinerators is no easy task. Many grassroots groups have had to campaign for years to keep these facilities out of their communities. Activists must confront the fear that jobs will be lost if an industry is shut down. Government officials and community groups often support toxic burners because of promised economic development.

Although opposition has intensified, citizen groups have persevered. One of the most widely publicized efforts has been a campaign in East Liverpool, Ohio, which began in the early 1980s to prevent the operation of the largest hazardous waste incinerator. Waste Technologies Industries (WTI) constructed the incinerator on the banks of the Ohio River just a few hundred feet from a residential neighborhood and 1,100 feet from an elementary school. One EPA official reportedly was shocked to see the WTI incinerator so close to a school and thought the company should pay to move it.

Some East Liverpool residents, however, have welcomed the incinerator because it is the first new industry to be built in the community in years. It is considered a boost for the area's depressed economy. But grassroots groups fighting for environmental justice have long opposed WTI and other waste disposal industry giants such as Waste Management, Inc., Browning-Ferris Industries, and several other large corporations that have repeatedly violated environmental laws. Charges and fines against these companies are a matter of public record, as grassroots groups have consistently pointed out.

Activists also helped make hazardous waste burning in general and the incinerator at East Liverpool in particular issues for the administration of President Bill Clinton. Vice President Al Gore initiated an investigation of the East Liverpool incinerator, and in May 1993 the Clinton administration announced an eighteen-month ban on new hazardous waste burners. However, the Environmental Protection Agency allowed a test burn at the WTI incinerator in East

52

The Waste Technologies Industries plant (above) in
East Liverpool, Ohio, would be the largest hazardous waste
incinerator in the United States. The plant was scheduled to
open in the summer of 1992, but local residents organized
protests, citing its location near residences, an elementary
school, and the Ohio River. The protesters brought their
objections as far as the White House and President Clinton.

Liverpool. Afterward, even though the agency found that the incinerator failed to meet all regulations, officials allowed a one-year permit for burning.

A multiracial coalition of grassroots groups from Ohio, Pennsylvania, and West Virginia has continued the protest to halt operations of the nation's largest hazardous waste burner. Their banners and chants state their message clearly: "We refuse to die for WTI!"

Hundreds of other examples of grassroots actions against hazardous waste sites have been reported since the beginning of the 1990s. To highlight just a few:

- After a two-year struggle, members of a group calling itself People Opposing Pollution were able to prevent a cement manufacturer from burning hazardous waste at its kiln near Mobile, Alabama.
- Northern California Citizens Against Pollution and Industrial Toxics organized to educate Bay Area citizens about Dow Chemical's attempt to build a hazardous waste incinerator in the community. This group distributed 10,000 flyers in three languages to residents, some of whom angrily protested at a local permit hearing. Within weeks, Dow withdrew its application.
- Over a period of six years, hundreds of activists in Kettleman City, California, a Latino community of primarily migrant workers have opposed the construction of a hazardous waste incinerator in their midst.
- After several years of citizen protests against a hazardous waste incinerator in Arizona, the state government bought the burner from ENSCO, the company that built it, paying $42.5 million to prevent hazardous waste burning.

MULTIPLE HAZARDS

Hazardous waste dumps and incinerators are not the only toxic facilities that threaten the health and safety of the poor and powerless.

Residents of west Harlem, in New York City, for example have to live with a myriad of contaminants. A sewage plant that treats 180 million gallons of raw sewage a day borders the neighborhood for about eight blocks along the Hudson River and produces foul-smelling hydrogen sulfide, a gas known to cause respiratory and eye problems. Hundreds of city buses stream in and out of two depots in the neighborhood as do hundreds of garbage trucks that haul their trash to a nearby dumping site from which the garbage is transferred to river barges for disposal elsewhere. A six-lane highway and a commuter rail line also cut through this community. Exhaust emissions from the many heavy vehicles have contributed to high levels of air pollution and an extremely high rate of asthma and other respiratory illnesses among residents. And until 1991, ash and airborne mercury from a crematorium spewed across the neighborhood and into nearby apartments. The crematorium was shut down because of its poisonous emissions.

In 1987, two community activists, Vernice Miller and Peggy Shepard, cofounded West Harlem Environmental Action (WHE ACT), the first grassroots group in New York City launched by African Americans, to combat the environmental hazards in their community. WHE ACT leaders have no doubt that the hazards would not exist if the neighborhood were made up of affluent white residents. In fact, the sewage treatment plant was first planned for an area of Manhattan made up of wealthier white residents, but they organized political opposition and persuaded city officials to site the sewage treatment plant in west Harlem.

WHE ACT has made some progress in calling attention to the treatment plant's design problems, which apparently contribute to the noxious fumes. After years of complaints and public hearings, the New York City administration promised to make repairs. Finally as a result of pressure and legal actions, the group was awarded one million dollars by the state to be used to ameliorate the conditions in the community. But this is only a small first step in the attempt to reduce multiple sources of pollution.[2]

The North River Treatment Sewage Plant in West Harlem,
New York City, spreads a bad odor that extends for blocks.
The emissions are added to the fumes of auto traffic on
the highway below. Residents Peggy Shepherd and Vernice
Miller founded the first grassroots group launched by
African Americans to protest the plant and eventually
they won the court case they had brought.

In another area of the United States, a concentration of at least 125 petrochemical companies along the Mississippi River in Louisiana has created multiple hazards for residents of small towns within this corridor, known as "cancer alley." Toxic emissions from chemical companies owned by Union Carbide, Shell Oil, Monsanto, Dow Chemical, Georgia Gulf, Occidental, American Cyanamid, and other corporations have contaminated the air, water, and land.

Most of the residents, who are primarily of African American ancestry, can name half a dozen or more relatives and neighbors who have died or are dying of cancer. One woman said she could feel the chemicals in her throat on humid days. "It's almost like you can taste the odor. I go look at my toilets, and they look like I haven't cleaned them in a month. If that water's settling in toilets and lavatories like that, what's it doing to the bottom of my stomach, to my kidneys?" she asked.[3]

Some outside the community blame high rates of cancer on the smoking habits and other lifestyle patterns of residents. But not all of the cancer victims have been smokers, and people who have lived in the area for most of their lives say that cancer was not prevalent years ago. In those days people died of old age or of strokes and heart attacks.

Residents are convinced that the contaminated air (and water) are killing them. As evidence, they point to the fact that their garden plants shrivel and die after their property has been shrouded in dense, foglike concentrations of air pollutants from petrochemical industries.

In the view of Pat Bryant, executive director of the Gulf Coast Tenants Organization in New Orleans, which is part of a coalition of environmental justice groups in the South, petrochemical companies have deliberately located along the Mississippi corridor, and companies continue to try to site new plants in the vicinity. Bryant charges that the corporations have expected little opposition because the communities were built by slaves and former slaves. Bryant calls the companies' actions a classic example of environmental racism. Outside the corridor, most people give little thought to the effects of petrochemical emissions. In fact, the area is often called a national "sacrifice zone" because, as Bryant explained, "so many Americans have accepted . . . the concept of acceptable risk . . . [I]t is all right to refine the petroleum and have all these poisons coming out, because the products, the plastics, the Saran Wraps, the fuel that we need to run this industrial society have to be made. Their by-products are necessary things. The risks can be absorbed; the affluent in society won't have to be closely associated with the risks."[4]

Bryant long has called for a revamping of the acceptable risk policy in the United States so that those who are "dirt poor" do not have to be at greatest risk. Along with other grassroots leaders he has fought for the right of people of color to safe jobs, decent housing, health care, and education. Because of protests by his group and others, there have been some achievements.

For example, some petrochemical companies have bought entire towns so as to allow residents to move to safer, healthier environments. Buying up property is not necessarily a humanitarian gesture on the part of corporations, however. Rather, companies want to limit their liabilities—the monetary awards they might have to pay if they are sued by people who suffer health problems due to polluting industries.

Wherever people have protested toxic emissions and hazardous waste disposal sites, there have been common demands: to keep toxic materials out and to reduce the amount of poisonous waste produced. Most grassroots efforts also oppose deliberate dumping of hazardous materials on low-income, blue-collar, rural, and people-of-color communities. While such efforts can be prolonged and difficult and even dangerous, they continue. Once organized, people feel empowered and able to express their views, with the hope that elected officials will act to protect their health and the health of their families and neighbors.

5
TOXIC THREATS TO NATIVE AMERICAN LANDS

Perhaps no protest sign has stated the environmental racism case more succinctly than one protesting an asbestos dump on a Native American reservation in New Mexico. It read: "We don't have the complexion for protection." The woman carrying the sign, a Navajo elder, was part of a growing grassroots movement among Native Americans that is demanding protection from toxic threats to Indian lands.

A number of investigative reports in recent years have shown that lands on American Indian reservations from Alaska to Florida have been trashed in some way, and have been polluted by industrial and medical waste and radioactivity. For example, industrial waste dumped into the Saint Lawrence River has contaminated fishing waters in Mohawk territory on both sides of the Canadian–United States border. Uranium tailings from mines on Navajo lands have blown across parts of the southwestern United States, turning some areas into radioactive sand dunes. Oil drilling, mining, logging, and other industrial activities have destroyed many Indian lands in the Northwest. Waste management companies have tried to construct toxic waste dumps and nuclear waste sites on reservations, assuming that impoverished tribes would accept multimillion-dollar offers for their land.

Some Native Americans have organized to fight back and are working to protect treaty rights established years ago. In 1991 representatives of fifty-seven different tribes and reservations formed the Indigenous Environmental Network in order to disseminate information and provide legal help concerning toxic threats.

Yet not all tribal elders have turned down offers of economic benefits in exchange for allowing toxic dump sites on reservations. Some tribal leaders have accepted financial payments for land that will be used for waste disposal. As a result even more controversy over toxic dumping has erupted among Native Americans, dividing some tribal groups.

INDIGENOUS PEOPLE AND TRIBAL GOVERNMENTS

Four major groups of indigenous people live in the continental United States and in insular (island) areas over which the U.S. government has some type of jurisdiction. These include Native Hawaiians, residents of 220 native villages in Alaska, and people living on 2,000 islands such as American Samoa and Guam. Well over 300 Native American tribes live on 280 separate reservations in the United States, including Metlakatla on Annette Island, Alaska. Although the U.S. government holds Native American lands in trust, each reservation has its own tribal government and operates as a semi-sovereign nation. Tribal leaders have responsibility for managing the environment within their reservations.

Recent U.S. laws have included provisions that allow a tribal government to set up environmental regulations for an Indian nation and to work cooperatively with the EPA, much as state governments do. Thus since the 1980s, tribal and insular governments have been able to take a more active role in managing their environmental resources. Many have had to deal with increased threats to natural resources, including efforts to site hazardous and solid waste treatment and disposal facilities on their lands.

However, few tribal governments have the needed personnel to oversee and protect natural resources. Many tribes also suffer severe poverty, with unemployment rates ranging from 65 to 85 percent among some groups. As a result, waste disposal companies, knowing that tribes desperately need jobs and capital, try to persuade tribal leaders to accept large-scale waste disposal facilities on reservations. In addition, many waste disposal companies know that if they can site facilities on reservations, they can circumvent stricter state environmental regulations. One common state requirement is an expensive environmental impact statement—a study to determine the effect a waste site will have on the environment.

DEBATES OVER RESERVATION DUMPING

Within the past decade, waste disposal companies have repeatedly approached tribal leaders in California, Arizona, Oklahoma, New York, and South Dakota with plans for large-scale garbage and hazardous waste disposal sites. Companies have solicited the Mohawk of New York State and Canada nearly a dozen times, for example. In many instances, tribal members and leaders have taken a strong stand against waste dumping on their land, but they have had to resist tempting offers.

One example is an industry offer that was made to leaders of a Lakota tribe (called the Sioux by outsiders) on the Pine Ridge Reservation in South Dakota, one of the poorest areas in the United States. In the fall of 1989, Amcor, a subsidiary of O&G, a waste disposal company based in Connecticut, promised jobs and cash payments in exchange for permission to dump trash on the reservation.

61

The Pine Ridge Indian Reservation (above) in South Dakota.
Joann Tall, who lives on the reservation, formed the
Native Resources Coalition to oppose the placement of
a hazardous waste disposal project at Pine Ridge.

Negotiations were kept secret from tribal members, but activist Joann Tall, who lives on the Pine Ridge Reservation and has spent years fighting for social and environmental justice for her people, learned about the plan. She formed a group called the Native Resource Coalition to oppose the waste disposal project.

In June 1990, Tall was informed that Amcor was entertaining tribal leaders at a luncheon at the Rapid City Hilton. She "crashed the meeting," as she put it, and began to ask Amcor representatives questions about the proposed waste disposal operation. "A tribal councilwoman accused me of being disrespectful," Tall reported.[1]

But she was not deterred and told the tribal leaders that they were being "sold out" with the big meal and other enticements, similar to the way Native Americans were disarmed with whiskey and persuaded to give up their land long ago. Tall urged tribal leaders to take responsibility to protect tribal rights and to do their own research.

Not long after the meeting, tribal leaders learned that many other Native American groups were being similarly enticed by waste disposal companies. Tribal leaders broke off negotiations with Amcor and refused to accept an agreement that required them to waive their sovereign rights. O&G then turned to the neighboring Rosebud Reservation, sending a representative from another subsidiary of the company.

There, as in Pine Ridge, negotiations with the Rosebud Tribal Council were conducted behind closed doors. In spite of objections from many of the six hundred residents of the Rosebud Reservation, the tribal council in late 1990 signed a contract with the waste disposal company to develop a 5,760-acre regional landfill. The proposed site would accept hazardous and solid waste from such major cities as Minneapolis and Denver, as well as other urban areas in the region.

According to Senator Thomas A. Daschle of South Dakota, who serves on the U.S. Senate's Select Committee on Indian Affairs, the firm had never before developed or operated a waste disposal site, but its contract stated in part: "In no event shall any environmental regulations or standards of South Dakota be applicable to this project." It further prohibited the Sioux from enacting new laws to govern the waste project. The only regulation would come from the EPA, which has never had sufficient funding or staff to properly oversee waste dumps.

The contract also stipulated that the disposal firm, not the tribe, would have "sole discretion" to determine content of materials dumped at the site and to monitor the quality of groundwater running beneath the site. If the tribe attempted to develop environmental standards to protect its people more fully than provided for by EPA regulations, the tribe would be forced to compensate the disposal firm for any profits lost on account of the new standards. What kind of compensation would the Sioux receive? They would be paid slightly over one dollar a ton to accept other people's garbage, which they would have to live with forever, Senator Daschle reported.[2]

Yet the plan to site the waste dump on the Rosebud Reservation did not materialize. Opponents of the dump—known as the Good Road Coalition—along with the Native Resource Coalition helped defeat the proposal. The plan was presented to the council again in 1992. But it was rejected once more.

AN ASBESTOS CONTROVERSY

In 1992 another waste disposal company called ICU applied for a permit to bury 50,000 cubic yards of asbestos waste on private land in northwestern New Mexico. The site selected was near Huerfano Mountain, at a mesa that Navajo people consider sacred. The proposed waste site would not only desecrate a sacred place but would also likely pose a health hazard to people living in the area.

Asbestos occurs naturally in the environment, and millions of tons of the mineral have been mined and used in insulating materials manufactured for more than a century. Because asbestos resists heat and many chemicals, it also has been widely used in vehicle brakes and clutches. In spite of its many practical benefits, however, asbestos is a hazardous material. The EPA banned its use for insulation in 1979 and in 1986 prohibited its use in many other products. Yet there are countless tons of asbestos materials still

*A waste site proposed near this
mesa would pose a health hazard to the
Navajo people living in the area.*

around in old buildings, machinery, ships, cars, and various types of equipment.

Airborne asbestos fibers are like tiny glass slivers that can be inhaled. Once in the lungs, asbestos remains there and can cause asbestosis, a disease that causes lumps and scarring, stiffening the lungs and making breathing difficult. Asbestos also causes lung cancer.

The dangers of asbestos have been widely publicized in recent years, but the hazards have been well known since at least the 1930s. For decades, companies producing asbestos and using it in manufacturing did not report on X rays of workers' lungs and studies showing that anywhere from 50 to 85 percent of workers exposed to asbestos developed lung diseases, which were often fatal.

When the asbestos disposal site was proposed for New Mexico, many people believed that the hazardous material would be buried "out of sight, out of mind," as the old saying goes. The disposal company's plans called for the asbestos to be wrapped in two plastic layers, each no thicker than an ordinary garbage bag, and covered with a layer of dirt three feet deep.

Peter Montague, an expert on hazardous waste and founder of the Environmental Research Foundation in Washington, D.C., predicted that the soil would erode and eventually the "plastic baggies of asbestos [would] be exposed to the sun." Once exposed, the plastic would "degrade rapidly, and then large quantities of asbestos fibers [would blow] throughout the region." In an issue of his highly respected weekly newsletter, Montague explained that "prairie dogs or other natural forces may disrupt the site much sooner and release the deadly asbestos." In his view, "The only real solution to [asbestos dumping] is to store asbestos in steel-reinforced concrete buildings built above-ground where they can be observed continually."[3]

Armed with such information and determined to save sacred land, a grassroots group called Diné CARE (Diné is a Navajo word for "the people") organized several protests against the asbestos waste site. Only a few people attended the first two public hearings on the project, which were held thirty miles from the Navajo reservation. But Diné CARE helped set up a third hearing near the dump site and brought in representatives of several other organizations.

After ICU presented its proposition, taking up a full day of testimony in an attempt to discourage opposing views, volunteers were able on the second day to present their case against the asbestos dump. Even before the volunteers had finished speaking, the company withdrew its application to place the dump site on the reservation. No one, however, expects this to be the last time the grassroots group will have to fight proposals for dumping toxic materials on Indian land.

LETHAL RADIOACTIVE CONTAMINANTS

Another type of battle against hazardous materials has been waged on reservations. It focuses on the disproportionate number of Native Americans exposed to radioactive contaminants, which social activists consider a form of genocide perpetrated by federal and state governments and the nuclear industry. In recent years, for example, residents of Point Hope, Alaska, who are primarily Inuit, discovered that in 1962 the U.S. government secretly buried 15,000 tons of radioactive soil near their village. The contaminated soil, including nuclear material from the bomb-testing site in Nevada, was placed in a dozen separate pits to determine how radioactivity spreads in an Arctic environment.

Later the nuclear material was buried in a pit four feet deep and covered with a mound of clean dirt. But no warnings of radioactive materials were posted. Thus, Point Hope residents unaware of any possible environmental hazards continued their hunting, herding, and gathering practices. Today residents have an above-average cancer rate, which for years was blamed on smoking and diet but is now linked to the radioactive soil.[4]

The Texas Department of Health placed this marker on
the 750 acres of ranchland contaminated by uranium
mill tailings from mining for weapons production.

Indigenous people recruited for uranium mining were similarly uninformed and unsuspecting victims of exposure to radioactivity. This situation was described in a 1993 story in the *New York Times*.

Almost fifty years ago, government engineers marched into Cove, Arizona, and urged young Navajo men and boys to put down the tools of sheepherding and farming and take up mining drills and dynamite in the nuclear defense of the nation. The government promised good wages but, federal records show, did nothing to warn the men of the excessive levels of radiation in the uranium mines.[5]

Uranium miners were recruited not only in Arizona but also in Colorado, New Mexico, Utah, and Wyoming. In the 1950s the federal government acknowledged that many of the miners developed lung cancer or other respiratory diseases because of exposure to high levels of radon, a radioactive gas produced from the decay of radium in uranium ore. In some families three or four members have died of lung cancer.

None of the miners were warned about the radon hazards until the late 1960s. Government officials claimed that their silence was justified because of "national security" and the "need for uranium," according to the *Times* report. After years of court battles and hearings before the U.S. Congress, the United States formally apologized in 1990. The federal government also set up a program to compensate the families of miners who were injured or killed by radiation in the federal mines. The compensation program is being administered by the U.S. Justice Department.

In order to receive compensation, families have to provide records of their health, work, and family history. But families who follow tribal custom do not keep written records, and the U.S. government and mining companies did not maintain detailed information about miners during the 1940s and 1950s. Some who are applying for compensation—among them men who worked in the mines and are now dying of cancer—do not read or speak English. All of these factors create obstacles and long delays in payments to victims and families of victims.

In the opinion of Stewart Udall, a former U.S. Secretary of the Interior who lives in the Southwest and serves as legal counsel for many Navajo, the federal government has created "a bureaucratic legal maze designed to prevent compensation. . . . There's no pity for what happened to these people. No understanding. You have a compassionate program administered in an utterly uncompassionate manner."[6]

DEBATES OVER NUCLEAR WASTE DUMP SITES

Another U.S. government program that could expose Native Americans to radioactive materials is the effort of the Department of Energy to site monitor-retrievable storage depositories—temporary, aboveground, radioactive waste dumps—on reservations. In 1991, the Energy Department, which oversees nuclear research and development, decided to try to revitalize the nuclear power industry. No new nuclear power plants had been put into operation for years, primarily because of widespread fear of radioactive waste and radioactive contamination of areas around nuclear power plants. At least twenty nuclear power plants have been shut due to the high cost of making needed repairs to cracked tubing, corroded pipes, and other reactor problems. Another two dozen nuclear reactors may close by the year 2000 because of high maintenance costs.

High-level radioactive wastes from power plants are inside fuel rods that must be replaced every few years. The used fuel rods will remain highly radioactive for many thousands of years, so disposal is a major problem. The rods are placed in so-called temporary storage—in pools of water that act as a shield against radiation, or the radioactive materials are placed in steel canisters that are stored in underground or aboveground sites.

Highly radioactive spent fuel and other nuclear wastes have been accumulating for years at power plants and nuclear weapons facilities. Yucca Mountain in Nevada, which the Shoshone people have long claimed is legally theirs, is being developed as the world's first permanent underground site for radioactive waste. But there have been many delays in construction, because engineers, geologists, and others have debated the safety of the site. Some are convinced there are insurmountable technical problems that will result in radioactive leaks. One study prepared for the federal government by Engineers International of Westmont, Illinois ("Assessment of Retrieval Alternatives for the Geological Disposal of Nuclear Waste") in 1983 indicated that Department of Energy designs for the site were flawed.

If no permanent storage facility can be developed for nuclear wastes, plants that reach their capacity to store radioactive material on site will have to be shut down. Consequently, the Department of Energy came up with a plan to offer grants of $100,000 to communities that would accept high-level nuclear waste on a temporary basis—up to forty years—until the waste can be moved to a permanent storage area.

But few people want those storage areas in their backyard, and community after community has protested the siting of nuclear storage dumps within its boundaries. Opponents of the plan argue that once the waste is sited in an area, it may become an immovable hazardous fixture. Nevertheless, by mid-1993, two counties and at least fourteen Native American tribes had accepted grants for nuclear waste storage.

Since the early 1990s, Mdewakanton Sioux (Dakota) in Prairie Island, Minnesota, have been in the middle of a major controversy over the possibility of a nuclear waste site near or within the reservation. The Northern States Power (NSP) company of Minnesota has operated a nuclear power plant less than half a mile from the reservation since the 1970s, storing increasing amounts of radioactive waste within the plant. In 1991 the power company applied to the Department of Energy for permission to store waste outside the plant in metal containers 16.5 feet tall and 8.5 feet in diameter. The casks would have radiation shielding and would be set on a concrete pad surrounded by an earth berm.[7]

Native Americans and other activists opposed the waste site, arguing that the site eventually would be used for nuclear waste from other parts of the United States. Activists tried to run a paid television commercial calling attention to NSP's plans to build new nuclear waste storage at the site and asking the public to express their opinions. But all the major television stations in the Minneapolis–Saint Paul area refused to run the ad. And state officials supported NSP's plans to increase the amount of nuclear waste next to the reservation, even though NSP admitted that it had never studied the health effects of nuclear waste on the neighboring Indian people. Neither had NSP ever conducted a study to determine whether Prairie Island was an adequate site for high-level nuclear waste.

In another effort to stop the waste disposal site, the tribe passed an ordinance requiring NSP to get a tribal license before it could haul waste through the reservation. But a federal judge issued a restraining order, which prevented the tribe from enforcing the ordinance.

After months of frustration, the Prairie Island tribal council decided that the only way to get away from NSP's nuclear plant was to notify the federal government that they would be willing to consider bringing all the U.S. nuclear waste to their reservation in return for millions of dollars to move the reservation elsewhere.

As one tribal council member, Lu Taylor-Jacobson, argued: "Since Northern States Power and the state of Minnesota seem committed to forcing our people to live next to high-level nuclear waste for an undetermined amount of time without any compensation, why shouldn't we become the national waste site? At least then we will be getting something for the dangers we are already being forced to live with."[8] The only compensation the tribe has received is $164 paid more than twenty years ago for the right to use a road through the reservation. (The nearby city of Red Wing, on the other hand, receives over $12 million each year in property taxes from the NSP plant.)

In 1992 the case again went to court, and an administrative court judge recommended that the state legislature vote to approve the application, which is legally required if the storage is to be permanent. The power company appealed the decision, but in mid-1993 the appeals court let the recommendation stand.

Meanwhile, the Prairie Island tribal council withdrew its application for a federal grant to store nuclear waste on the reservation, because it seemed that the NSP would not be allowed to build its nuclear waste containers near Indian land. Yet tribal leaders said they would keep their options open, since the NSP is appealing to the Minnesota Supreme Court to reverse the decision against its nuclear waste site.[9]

6

POISONING WITH PESTICIDES

More than thirty years ago, naturalist Rachel Carson wrote *Silent Spring,* a book warning of the dangers of pesticides—manufactured chemicals that kill organisms harmful to food crops and other vegetation. Carson's book documented how overuse of DDT, a pesticide that is now banned, and other agricultural chemicals killed far more than pests. The poisons also destroyed and maimed many birds and other wildlife beneficial to the environment. Her book revealed that manufactured toxic substances can upset nature's ecosystems—areas of the environment in which plants and animals are interrelated and depend on one another for survival.

Some attempts were made in the 1960s and 1970s to reduce the use of toxic agrochemicals, as chemical pesticides and fertilizers are now called. But giant agricultural corporations that produce much of the U.S. food supply have continued to apply vast amounts of pesticides, as have home gardeners, lawn-care and pest-control professionals, and others. These poisonous chemicals include insecticides that kill insects, fungicides that destroy fungi and molds, herbicides that destroy weeds, nematocides that kill nematodes (small soil worms), and rodenticides that kill rodents.

There is little doubt that over the past fifty years, pesticides have helped U.S. growers increase agricultural production. Indeed, many agricultural corporations that have supported the widespread use of pesticides claim that without agrochemicals severe food shortages and famine will occur. They also predict that prices for food will soar.

But the abuse of pesticides has exacted a heavy toll. Pesticide exposure has caused serious health problems among various groups in the population, particularly those who work with the poisons. More than one hundred pesticides are known carcinogens (cancer-causing substances), and at least seventy-one of these pesticides are used on food crops. Pesticides also have been linked to birth defects, respiratory problems, and other disabilities.

CALLS FOR REDUCING PESTICIDE USE

In May 1993, two activist groups, the World Wildlife Fund and Public Voice for Food and Health Policy, released reports indicating that U.S. agrochemical use is steadily increasing while European countries are significantly reducing pesticide use. The groups urged the U.S. government to adopt an ambitious national strategy to reduce dependence on pesticides and other agrochemicals.

A month later, the Natural Resources Defense Council (NRDC), a national organization that conducts scientific studies on environmental problems, issued one of several reports on pesticides that NRDC has published over the years. Titled "After *Silent Spring:* The Unsolved Problems of Pesticide Use in the United States," the report showed that over two billion pounds of pesticides are applied annually—eight pounds for every person in the United States— double the amount used in the 1960s. In addition, the report stated that 440,000 wells and 10 percent of other sources of water in the United States are contaminated

This airplane is spreading pesticides over the crops. Pesticides contain carcinogens and as a result farmworkers have a high incidence of cancer.

with pesticides. Poisonous pesticide residues also have been found on 38 percent of food samples analyzed by the federal government. In addition to ingesting pesticides in water and on food, many people have been exposed to heavy doses of pesticides sprayed from planes, trucks, or hand-held equipment.[1]

On June 29, 1993, a four-year study conducted by the

acclaimed National Academy of Sciences was released. As other researchers concluded years earlier, the fourteen-member academy panel found that some infants and children may be ingesting unsafe amounts of pesticide residues on fruits and vegetables, because they consume more of these foods and the pesticides on them in proportion to their body weight than adults do. The current method for determining pesticide risk is based on the average exposure of a population, which the panel found seriously deficient in terms of evaluating the toxic effects of pesticides, especially the occurrence of cancer, in children.[2]

In the study titled "Pesticides in the Diets of Infants and Children," researchers pointed out that "Infants and children are subject to rapid tissue growth and development, which will have an impact on cancer risk." But the panel said fruits and vegetables should be part of children's diet and that "washing and peeling fruits and vegetables will go a long way toward reducing risk."[3]

After the panel report was made public, the EPA, the USDA, and the U.S. Food and Drug Administration jointly called for reductions in the use of chemicals on fruits and vegetables. The National Agricultural Chemical Association representing pesticide manufacturers promised to cooperate in efforts to ensure food safety. However, a week earlier the association had argued against NRDC's report, stating that the use of insecticides, considered one of the most dangerous pesticides, had "decreased by two-thirds since 1966."[4]

PROTESTS OVER PESTICIDE SPRAYING

Many people are exposed to dangerous pesticides because they live near areas that are sprayed with insecticides, herbicides, and other poisonous chemicals. Some people have severe reactions to pesticides, as a mother in Arizona explained a few years ago. Her two sons had played outdoors after a pesticide spraying around their home, and within

77

three days the oldest boy "began having convulsions, with profuse sweating, chest congestion, and glazed eyes. . . . Both boys developed ulcers inside their nostrils. And our two dogs, who live in the back yard, became very ill with the same symptoms of seizures and open sores on their skin."[5]

Those who oppose widespread pesticide use call it another form of exploitation of those least able to defend themselves. But grassroots groups have formed to demand protection. For example, in many parts of the United States, parents have joined together to block the use of pesticides around schools and on school playgrounds.

In northern California, a group called Mow Our Weeds (MOW) fought for eleven years to persuade the California Department of Transportation to mow the roadsides rather than spray herbicides to control weeds along scenic Highway 1. The group began its protest after a highway truck sprayed poisons on blackberries that people living in the area picked and ate. In 1992, the herbicide spraying stopped along Highway 1, but MOW plans to continue its battle to reduce the 400,000 gallons of herbicides sprayed along California highways each year.

Not all activist efforts succeed, however. During the summer of 1992, the Native Resource Coalition of South Dakota's Pine Ridge Reservation hoped to stop the spraying of 12,000 gallons of the insecticides carbaryl and dimilin to control a grasshopper infestation on 80,000 acres of Oglala Sioux land. But the Oglala Sioux Tribe Executive Committee and the U.S. Bureau of Indian Affairs favored the spraying.

The Sioux leaders approved the spraying on the advice of the U.S. Department of Agriculture, which is charged with controlling grasshopper infestations on public and private lands. At a later public meeting, however, the Native Resource Coalition presented information to tribal leaders about the toxicity of the two insecticides that would be used.

Carbaryl (Sevin 4-oil), one of the most widely applied

insecticides in the United States, has been linked with birth defects; damages to the kidney, liver, ovaries, and testes; and behavioral problems in humans and animals. Children, pregnant women, the elderly, and people in poor health are especially vulnerable to carbaryl's effects. Acute signs and symptoms of carbaryl poisoning include blurred vision, nausea, headache, breathing difficulties, and muscle twitching.

Dimilin prevents insect growth, attacking larva and eggs. The insecticide is not registered for use on grasshoppers, but an experimental use permit was issued to spray 1,280 acres of the Pine Ridge Reservation. Some Oglala tribe members along with the National Coalition Against the Misuse of Pesticides (NCAMP) were convinced that the grasshopper infestation on Oglala tribal land was being used as a pretext for the Department of Agriculture and insecticide manufacturers to test more widespread use of dimilin. According to Susan Cooper of NCAMP, even though Agriculture Department officials knew "that the grasshoppers were adult . . . they sprayed the test plots with dimilin . . . [which] is utterly ineffective against adult insects."[6]

After the public meeting, tribal President John Yellow Bird Steele sent a letter to the Bureau of Indian Affairs, reversing the decision of his executive committee and canceling the spraying. At the same time, the Native Resource Coalition obtained a temporary restraining order in tribal court to halt the spraying pending further investigation of possible toxic effects. Since the Bureau of Indian Affairs is not legally bound by the tribal court, the agency ignored the restraining order and allowed the USDA to spray the insecticides.

Bill and Emily Koenen of the Native Resource Coalition, who were attending a religious ceremony when the spraying began, reported that "The carbaryl smelled like burned rubber and you could see a layer of brown fog across the land."[7] The Koenens also expressed concern that the sprayings, which took place during a period of heavy rainfall, contaminated water runoff and groundwater. Later some of the participants in the ceremonies reported symptoms of insecticide poisoning.

EXPLOITATION OF HIRED FARMWORKERS

As a group, those most affected by pesticide use are the people who plant, cultivate, and harvest fruits and vegetables: farmers and hired farmworkers and their families. Of the approximately two million hired farmworkers, several hundred thousand are migrants who travel from one section of the country to another, following the planting and harvesting cycles in North America.

Hired farmworkers often "labor under the worst conditions of any group of workers in the United States," according to Marion Moses, a physician with many years of experience treating pesticide-related health problems. In an essay on environmental racism, she explained that farmworkers "suffer from many kinds of toxic exposure and a paucity of legal protections. Their neglect by most mainstream environmental organizations is a political scandal."[8]

Since the 1960s when CBS produced a network TV special called "Harvest of Shame," other TV documentaries, books, news reports, and numerous magazine features have focused on the plight of migrant farmworkers. It is a group made up primarily of Spanish-speaking people and people of color who have long been used and abused as a source of cheap labor.

Many in U.S. society believe that hiring minority people for farm labor is necessary to maintain the agricultural economy, because white workers will not accept farm labor jobs, and that the work provides income for people who otherwise would have none. There is little doubt that farmworkers from Mexico, for example, have few opportunities for jobs and will tolerate working conditions that may be better than they can find in Mexico. But U.S. farm labor

80

conditions are strikingly inferior to the standards set for other industries. The problem has been part of the American social structure and economy for many decades. As Marion Moses stated: "The exploitation of ethnic minorities in agriculture is deeply rooted in American history."[9]

Moses traced the racist pattern of agriculture's dependence on cheap labor, beginning with the enslavement of millions of Africans and Native Americans for forced labor on plantations. The indenture system also provided a labor pool for agriculture. A great number of immigrants were indentured servants, working to pay off debts for ship passage to America.

During the late 1800s and early 1900s, Asian immigrants were brought to the United States to become part of the low-wage, agricultural labor pool. These workers were replaced by poor white families during the Great Depression of the 1930s. Then World War II brought jobs for many Americans and excluded Asians, particularly Japanese Americans, from the labor force. Growers began to import Mexican farmworkers, who are now a major part of the agricultural industry in the West and the Southwest.[10]

CURRENT FARMWORKER PROBLEMS

As in the past, today's hired farmworkers in the United States are predominantly people of color, and the workers along with their families face serious health hazards due in part to the lack of protective laws and the efforts by some growers to circumvent whatever regulations are in place. A report by the *Los Angeles Times* in 1993 highlighted a number of examples. One was the effort by growers to bring back the legally banned short-handled hoe for weeding and cultivating. The implement was banned because workers using the hoe had to constantly labor in a stooped position. Some growers have required workers to weed by hand in an attempt to create a demand for the hoe.

In other cases, employers have routinely withheld workers' pay, according to advocacy groups such as the California Rural Legal Assistance, which represents workers. The *Los Angeles Times* reported that "makeshift camps where workers live in squalor beside streams and in caves have proliferated, in part due to a steep decrease in the amount of employer-provided housing" and also because government agencies are "thinly staffed" and unable to enforce protective laws. Child-labor laws also have been violated, and young children who should be in elementary school have been found working alongside their parents in the fields.

Another example of farmworker exploitation is the increasing number of middlemen who contract with growers to supply laborers. According to the *Times* report, these contractors are likely to charge workers "exorbitant fees for everything from rent to transportation to sodas in the field. In many cases, workers must purchase such services in order to be hired."[11]

Farm labor advocates say workers face transportation hazards as well. Employers or contractors frequently arrange transport for workers to fields and groves. Workers travel long distances in poorly maintained and overcrowded vehicles. Since the beginning of the 1990s, unsafe farm trucks and buses in Florida and Georgia reportedly have been involved in numerous accidents, causing serious injuries and deaths among laborers.

In 1992, a report from the U.S. General Accounting Office, the investigative arm of the U.S. Congress, noted that many hired laborers work in fields without drinking water, hand-washing facilities, or toilets. When workers do not have sufficient drinking water, they become dehydrated or suffer from other heat-related problems. Lack of water for hand washing leads to the spread of communicable diseases and allows pesticide residues to remain on workers' skin.[12]

Each year, tens of thousands of hired farmworkers suffer illnesses due to pesticide exposure. No one knows the exact number of poisonings because victims often do not seek medical care. If they do, doctors may fail to diagnose poisonings accurately—symptoms are often similar to those associated with the flu. However, it is clear that farmworkers have died because of exposure to some highly toxic pesticides such as ethyl parathion. On the market since the 1950s, parathion has been used on about fifty crops in California. "Between 1982 and 1988, there were 124 illnesses in California either caused by or linked to ethyl parathion exposure," according to a *Los Angeles Times* report. The newspaper also noted that "the pesticide poisoned 648 people in the United States" during the period from 1966 to 1988. "Of those victims, 463 required hospitalization and 99 died."[13] Parathion is now banned for most agricultural uses, although it is applied to some crops harvested by machine.

Over the years, there have been numerous reports of farmworkers being sprayed with pesticides while planting or harvesting in the fields. Federal regulations require that workers stay out of a field for a specific length of time after spraying, but those rules are not always followed, and workers are not warned about the dangers of spraying.

In the summer of 1992, about one hundred migrant workers in Georgia were accidentally sprayed with a fungicide called chlorothalonil, used to protect peanut crops. Those exposed to chlorothalonil may suffer eye irritation, skin rashes, or breathing difficulties.

One of the Georgia farm owners who ordered the spraying said he forgot the workers were in the field. He later insisted that the incident had been blown out of proportion by the media, since news reports called the chemical spray a pesticide rather than a fungicide, which of course is one type of pesticide. The owner went on to claim that the fungicide probably would not hurt the workers.[14]

A fungicide called Benlate DF, which is widely used in greenhouses and on some nursery farms, is another pesticide that has been cited for toxic effects. In 1993, some farm owners in Alabama, Georgia, Florida, Hawaii, and Michigan filed lawsuits against Du Pont Company, the manufacturer of the product. Growers charged that the fungicide

Farmworkers are harvesting lettuce. In the Southwest and the West, farmworkers are primarily Hispanics and are exposed to many forms of pesticides. The United Farm Workers union organized a boycott of agricultural products to stop the use of pesticide spraying that was endangering its members.

created a toxic effect on plants, destroying millions of dollars' worth of crops. According to agricultural officials, the worst damage occurred in Florida where about one million dollars' worth of plants were destroyed.

Prior to the growers' lawsuit, the Farmworkers Association of Central Florida had accused Florida growers of "exposing thousands of farmworkers and their families throughout the state to this deadly substance [Benlate].

Exposure has occurred without notification or the recourse to appropriate health services," the farmworkers stated, adding that they would "no longer tolerate" this health threat. "Preliminary research on the effects of exposure to [Benlate] . . . has revealed that miscarriages, testicular cancer, nosebleeds, temporary blindness, dizziness and other severe health problems can result," the farmworkers noted.[15]

THE STRUGGLE FOR RIGHTS
AND PROTECTION

Some religious organizations, civil rights groups, a few government agencies, and some farm owners have tried for decades to improve the living and working conditions of hired farmworkers. One well-known leader in this effort was the late Cesar Chavez, who died in April 1993. A mythic figure, Chavez struggled most of his adult life for farmworkers' rights and social justice.

Chavez was the son of a migrant worker and had been a farmworker himself during the 1950s and 1960s. He knew that Mexican workers at that time were powerless, unable to organize strikes against unfair labor practices. Workers worried about losing what little money they could make— they earned an average of $1.50 per hour—since there were always other workers ready to take their place. They also feared reprisal; going out on strike frequently resulted in violence, imprisonment, and deportation.

Under Chavez's leadership, farmworkers organized the United Farm Workers in 1965. Chavez and the United Farm Workers called for a national boycott of table grapes, which millions of Americans joined. The boycott lasted for five years and eventually forced growers to sign union contracts guaranteeing workers fair wages and medical and unemployment benefits. Chavez led a second grape boycott in 1988 to protest the heavy use of pesticides in vineyards and to demand greater protection for workers. To publicize the boycott, Chavez fasted for thirty-six days, nearly dying as a result.

Still, farmworkers in the United States continue to face pesticide hazards as well as other health threats. And activists continue to fight for farmworker protection. One such person is Mary Ellen Beaver, a grandmother who works as a paralegal—a lawyer's assistant—for the Florida Rural Legal Services. In spite of threats of physical violence from employers, middlemen, and others who exploit workers, Beaver has spent more than two decades among farmworkers in the Southeast, telling them how to exercise their rights and prevent abuse.

In other parts of the country, some farmworkers have filed lawsuits against federal agencies, such as the EPA, that have not enforced protective measures for workers. Other lawsuits have been filed against chemical companies that produce toxic pesticides.

One lawsuit filed during the 1980s was settled out of court in the summer of 1992. The suit was against Dow Corning and Shell Oil Company on behalf of one thousand banana plantation workers in Costa Rica, some of whom were sterilized by exposure to DBCP, a nematocide that was banned for most uses in the United States in 1979. (The poison was used on pineapple plantations in Hawaii until 1985, however.) The ban came about after revelations that thirty-five workers in an Occidental Chemical Company plant in the United States had been sterilized by their exposure to DBCP.

DBCP is also a potent carcinogen, and can cause numerous other acute and chronic health effects. But chemical companies did not release that information to the public. Thus the companies have been found liable for damages caused by the nematocide.

Another means of fighting pesticide exposure is to document the effects and educate workers and the public on the hazards. A farmworkers' group in Oregon known as Pineros y Campesinos Unidos del Noroeste is doing just that. In support of its effort, the group received a grant in 1992 for

$8,000 from Ben & Jerry's Foundation. The foundation was set up by the ice cream company of the same name to foster projects designed to better the lives of disadvantaged people and to protect the environment.[16]

In the spring of 1993, the EPA, the National Cancer Institute, and the National Institute of Environmental Health Sciences announced a major study of the health of farm owners, farmworkers, and their families. A collaborative effort, the study will be conducted over a period of at least ten years.

The National Cancer Institute pointed out that farmers and hired farmworkers are exposed not only to pesticides but also to other toxins such as "chemical solvents, engine exhausts, animal viruses, and other substances common to agriculture." Prior studies have shown that farmers in the United States have higher than normal rates of several types of cancer, including skin cancers, certain kinds of leukemia, and cancers of the brain and prostate. The current study is expected to provide important data on the health effects on people who have had exposure to various hazardous materials.

Up to 100,000 male and female farmers, farmers' spouses, workers who apply agricultural pesticides, and their children will be part of the research effort. Although few studies of farmer health in the United States have compared the health status of various ethnic groups, the National Institute of Environmental Health Sciences noted that the jointly sponsored study will analyze two distinct groups: a group of Iowa farmers and farmworkers who are primarily white, and a group of North Carolina farmers and workers of predominantly Native American and African American descent.[17]

However, the current studies do not include Latino workers even though the vast majority of migrant and seasonal agricultural workers are Hispanic. The National Coalition of Hispanic Health and Human Services Organizations called the omission "abominable," although another study focusing on Hispanic farmworkers may be conducted at a later time.

REDUCING PESTICIDE USE

For years, many activists have been urging reduction of pesticide use as a protective measure rather than trying to control poisons after they have been produced. Some growers already practice one or more agricultural methods that cut back on chemical pesticides. One is integrated pest management (IPM), a system that makes use of pests' natural enemies—parasites, predators, and pathogens that destroy insects, fungi, weeds, and other organisms harmful to crops. Parasites live on other organisms, destroying them; predators prey on and attack other living things; and pathogens cause disease. In some cases, chemical pesticides are used in IPM strategy but usually as a last resort only.[18]

Some growers also use crop rotation, altering the crops grown in a field each year or planting two or three different crops in one field. When a single crop is grown, pests are more likely to gain a foothold, requiring heavy doses of chemical pesticides. Rotation discourages massive infestation of a pest that feeds on a specific crop.

A coalition of groups, including the Farmworker Justice Fund, the National Coalition Against the Misuse of Pesticides, and the National Audubon Society, is currently pressing for reform in agricultural practices nationwide. The coalition's overall goal is to reduce the reliance on pesticides generally and the use of the riskiest pesticides in particular.

Yet many activists fear that reductions will be hampered by manufacturers of agricultural chemicals, large corporations that control vast acres of farmland, and government officials who support agrochemical use. History has shown that change will not come quickly. The major hope of activists is that the American public will heed the call for social justice and in the very least demand that the powerless be protected from pesticide exposure, which in turn would benefit the general population.

7

BACKLASH AGAINST GRASSROOTS GROUPS

When grassroots groups confront environmental racism and seek justice for those who are exploited, they may be faced with a backlash. Usually that backlash comes from industry and government officials or from the middlemen who exploit farmworkers. Many activists have been harassed, threatened with violence, or even physically harmed. In a few cases, death has occurred from the physical violence. Activists also have been arrested, jailed, and sued for alleged civil violations.

Another type of backlash has developed among groups of small-business owners and industry representatives who have been pressing their demands for what they call "wise use" of the environment.

Those who support the wise use movement say they have a right to exploit the nation's natural resources and stop environmentalists who, in the opinion of wise use proponents, are more interested in insects and rodents than they are in people's welfare and in economic development.

MANY FORMS OF HARASSMENT

Harassment of grassroots activists takes many forms. In some cases there are attempts at intimidation. For example, in Richmond County, North Carolina, members of a grassroots group known as FORRCE (FOR Richmond County's Environment) held a meeting in early 1992 at a church. At the meeting, FORRCE members discussed their efforts to fight a low-level nuclear waste site proposed for the county. Although there was no indication that the meeting would be anything but orderly, the church was surrounded by state police officers in eighteen patrol cars, some cruising along a road nearby and others parked beside the church. "There was no reason for such a heavy police presence except to intimidate people," the chairman of the group said.[1]

Some industries and businesses that are polluters have used the old divide-and-conquer tactic as a form of harassment. Company representatives convince some workers that their fellow citizens are misinformed about hazardous materials and that those actively involved in protest efforts are jeopardizing jobs. Thus one employee group is pitted against another, which spills over into the community, dividing families and friends and sometimes leading to violence.

Harassment also has included invasion of privacy. Activists have reported that some businesses have hired private investigators to pry into the lives of grassroots leaders. The purpose is to search for information that will discredit activists and make their cause look suspect.

Another form of harassment is a negative propaganda campaign similar to the kind waged against political candidates. For example, representatives of some polluting industries have asserted that grassroots activists are zealots who distort facts or that activists are antibusiness and are attempting to terrorize communities across the United States.

Contributing to misleading propaganda are some talk-show personalities, journalists, government officials, and industry representatives who publicly ridicule people who

90

are trying to protect themselves from environmental hazards. For example, flamboyant Rush Limbaugh frequently blasts environmentalists on his TV show and radio program, and in his best-seller, *The Way Things Ought to Be*, Limbaugh accuses activists of being socialists and fanatics intent on destroying the American way of life.

Limbaugh's view appears to be in line with syndicated conservative columnists such as George Will. In a 1992 column, Will accused some environmentalists of having a political agenda and called environmentalism a "green tree with red roots" (akin to communism) and a "socialist dream."[2]

Editors of the *New American* magazine created a 1992 special issue in an attempt to show that environmentalists were a threat to society. Every article was designed to discount a specific environmental problem such as hazardous waste and water pollution, frequently presenting views of scientists who do not represent the majority of scientific experts studying environmental deterioration. The magazine's editorial accused environmentalists of having a "totalitarian agenda" and insisted that warnings about environmental decay were simply an attempt to justify "world government."[3]

BACKLASH FROM THE WISE USE MOVEMENT

Bashing environmentalists and grassroots activists is a common tactic among those who are part of the so-called wise use movement, which came into being in 1988. The effort began when a former environmental activist, Ron Arnold, joined forces with Alan Gottlieb, a fund-raiser for politically conservative causes who was convicted of income tax fraud when he was head of the Citizens Committee for the Right to Keep and Bear Arms in 1984.[4] The two created the Center for the Defense of Free Enterprise and set up their proposals for what they called wise use of natural resources, thus distorting a motto that was first applied in the 1800s.

At that time, conservationists used the term "wise use" to warn against exploitation of forests and other natural resources. In contrast to early conservation efforts, however, the wise use movement of today has launched anti-environmental campaigns, deliberately using tactics similar to those used by grassroots activists. Many groups in the wise use movement assert they are part of a grassroots effort and use names that foster that image, such as Alliance for America, Citizens for the Environment, Council for Solid Waste Solutions, National Wetlands Coalition, People for the West!, and Sahara Club. Their "environment-friendly" names, however, disguise the fact that the groups are made up primarily of representatives of major U.S. corporations and industry groups, and some are backed by leaders of the Unification Church of Sun Myung Moon, a Korean billionaire who often supports militant right-wing organizations.

People for the West!, for example, was established to maintain a federal law that allows mining companies to buy public land for a maximum of $5.00 per acre to exploit any mineral deposits found. As might be expected, the group receives large donations from mining and petroleum industries. Other groups are funded by such industry groups as the American Motorcyclists Association and the National Forest Products Association.[5]

Advocates of wise use say their primary goal is to maintain private property rights, which in their view have been eroded by environmental regulations. They want to open up public land, such as national parks and wilderness areas, to private use.

The wise use agenda stems from a biblical view that God wanted humans to "have dominion over . . . every living thing that moveth upon the earth" (Genesis 1:28). Some in the wise use movement accuse environmentalists of being antireligious—and specifically anti-Christian—in their refusal to accept the dominion-over-all philosophy. However, many religious groups, including the American Hebrew Congregations, the World Council of Churches, and the U.S. Catholic Conference, say this is a misguided view and is supplanted by biblical commands to be stewards of the earth. One biblical scholar said that "nature and wildlife were sources of inspiration for many of the prophets . . . and one cannot fully understand the Scriptures . . . without an appreciation for the natural environment that inspired so much of what appears therein. Although this is rarely preached from the pulpit, the Bible contains a message of conservation, respect for nature, and kindness to animals."[6]

Conservative religious advocates of the wise use movement, however, belittle the idea of preserving natural resources, since they believe that God will provide people with their basic needs now and in the hereafter. Thus they applaud such actions as clear-cutting the rapidly disappearing ancient forests in the Pacific Northwest, opening up national parks and wilderness areas to mining and oil drilling, and dismantling federal laws that protect endangered species. Some organizations such as the Sahara Club, a group of dirt-bike enthusiasts, have advocated violence against environmentalists and grassroots activists.[7]

The wise use movement is supported also by many small-business owners who blame their hard times on government regulations and other limits to business pursuits. John Roush, former chairman of the board of the Nature Conservancy, an environmental organization, explained this phenomenon at a convention of journalists in November 1992: "Government bureaucracies and environmentalists have not been sensitive to small land owners' needs and genuine concerns. A lot of 'wise use' leaders are opportunists and the environmental movement created some of those opportunities. The environmental movement has some work to do."[8]

This is clearly the case in the Adirondack Wilderness area of New York State, where some owners of small tracts of land want to be able to sell their property or develop it for tourism. Some of the land is in one of the poorest counties of New York where seasonal jobs pay only mini-

93

mum wage. The land is also under the jurisdiction of the state's Adirondack Park Agency, which was set up in 1971 to prevent haphazard development near Interstate 87. In 1990 the state legislature gave the agency control over land development along lakeshores and roads and in the back-country. But at least one thousand landowners formed an organization called the Adirondack Solidarity Alliance to protest—sometimes violently—what it called the dictator-ship of the Adirondack Park Agency. One of the leaders warned that "Adirondackers will be forced to live in con-centration camps working as slave laborers for the APA."[9]

Still, the majority of Adirondack area residents want to preserve the wilderness region, according to surveys. But conservationists are not always willing to speak out, particu-larly if they fear that they will be victims of violence. So the task at hand for environmental activists is to build "their own grassroots coalition" to support preservation, as one Audubon Society member noted.[10]

LEGAL ACTIONS: SLAPP AND
SLAPP-ING BACK

Certainly numerous business people in farming, timber, manufacturing, and other industries are concerned about natural resource preservation because their livelihood de-pends on access to raw materials. But those with financial investments in projects such as waste dumps, incinerators, and real estate development have frequently attempted to stop grassroots opposition with a legal tactic known as a Strategic Lawsuit Against Public Participation, or SLAPP. Using the SLAPP tactic, business and government officials can file lawsuits against opponents, charging them with business interference and loss of income, violation of civil or constitutional rights, and even conspiracy.

A few years ago, for example, a former policeman who is now a criminal justice instructor in Worcester, Massachu-setts, organized his neighbors to protest the expansion of a nearby airport. The neighborhood group wanted to protect wetlands and wildlife in the area and prevent contamination of their water supply. To stop the volunteer group, the city sued the former cop for $1.3 million. Although Worcester officials eventually dropped the lawsuit, the legal action caused great stress, pain, and fear for the neighborhood group. And that apparently is the point of SLAPPs—to intimidate citizens and to discourage opposition.

According to one attorney who has represented activists, "SLAPPs drive an absolute wedge between citizens and their representatives. They send a clear message that there is a 'price' for speaking out politically. The price is a multimillion dollar lawsuit and the expenses, lost resources and emotional stress such litigation brings."[11]

Yet many grassroots groups refuse to be silenced and are continuing their legal protests. When SLAPP actions have been taken against them, some groups have been vindicated by courts in Pennsylvania, Maryland, and Louisiana, to cite a few. Judges have declared SLAPP cases nonsuits, dismissing them as attempts to stifle public comment. As a result, in some instances grassroots groups have sought amends with SLAPP-back actions—countersuits of their own.

A case in point was a 1987 citizen suit in northern California's Contra Costa County. Alan LaPointe, a graphic designer in Richmond, organized a citizen group to oppose the sanitary district's planned waste incinerator. Every day the proposed incinerator would burn 1,000 tons of garbage, imported from Marin County, San Francisco, and Berkeley, to produce electrical power.

LaPointe and forty-nine other citizens brought suit against the sanitary district, primarily because the burner was planned for property six blocks from an elementary school. In addition, the sanitary district had diverted $5.9 million in funds earmarked for water projects to the incinerator project. (A grand jury later "determined that sanitary district officials [were] engaged in financial mismanagement and conflicts of interest," according to a legal news service report from BNA *California Environment Daily.* [12])

Although the district eventually dropped the incinerator project because the plan to sell electricity generated by the incinerator fell through, sewer district officials filed a countersuit against LaPointe. According to the attorney for the district, "They [officials] felt actions taken by Mr. LaPointe and others had gone beyond free speech rights" and that opponents had defamed sanitary district officials and interfered with business negotiations, which would result in a $42 million loss for the district.

LaPointe and his attorneys said that the countersuit was a SLAPP action designed to intimidate LaPointe and force him to drop his lawsuit. Had LaPointe's lawyers not provided services on a pro bono basis—without charge, to protect the public good—LaPointe, who had never before filed a lawsuit, would have had to borrow money to pay for his defense.

LaPointe decided to fight back because, in his words, "Part of the Constitution and the First Amendment is that citizens have the right to redress grievances. This is not a developer—it's my government." He felt the sanitary district SLAPP action was an affront to his "constitutional rights and to anyone who speaks out on a public issue." He said that if his own government could take such an action, then "we're in sad city." Thus LaPointe filed still another lawsuit, a SLAPP-back action, seeking damages for violation of his First Amendment rights: *LaPointe v. West Contra Costa County Sanitary District.*

The case was settled in October 1992 when a jury awarded LaPointe $205,100 in damages. It was the first jury award of its kind in the nation—a SLAPP-back award that many grassroots activists hope will discourage SLAPP actions by government officials against citizens who oppose them. As William Chapman, LaPointe's attorney, said, "It's bad enough when companies do this, but when your government does it, it's an outrage." [13]

8
A GLOBAL PROBLEM

While many U.S. citizens who once felt powerless are now organizing to protect themselves and their communities from industrial pollutants and toxic dumping, they also are emphasizing the motto: "Not in anyone's backyard." They adamantly oppose the exploitation and trashing of any group of people wherever they live.

The problem of dumping poisonous materials and endangering public health goes well beyond the borders of the United States. Since the beginning of the 1980s, the United States and other industrialized countries have been exporting increasing amounts of hazardous products. The sale of some of the exports, such as pesticides, asbestos, and leaded gasoline, is prohibited in the United States, but the products are shipped to countries that have few laws protecting public health. Exports of toxic trash from U.S. industries also go to so-called developing nations—less industrialized countries. In addition, U.S. corporations have been building factories in countries that need income and jobs—especially Mexico—where industrial regulations are few and those that do exist are not strictly enforced. As a result, corporations without fear of penalty pollute the land, water, and air of host countries and endanger the health of workers.

DUMPING BANNED PESTICIDES ABROAD

Although a variety of toxic products that are restricted or banned for use in the United States are exported overseas, the most widely condemned exports are highly toxic pesticides used in agriculture. Since pesticide residues remain on food products that are grown overseas and then imported into the United States, the pesticides come back to pose hazards for American consumers, creating what is known as "a circle of poison." The term was coined by David Weir and Mark Schapiro in *Circle of Poison*, published in 1981 by the Center for Investigative Reporting. In their book, the two investigative reporters documented how U.S. industries established international trade in pesticides that were restricted or banned in the United States.

Ten years later, the Foundation for Advancements in Science and Education (FASE) prepared the first detailed report of pesticide exports with data from U.S. Customs records. The report revealed that between March and May 1990 "American companies had exported U.S.-banned, unregistered, and restricted-use compounds at a rate of nearly three tons per hour."[1]

In the spring of 1993, FASE released findings from a second investigation of U.S. pesticide exports, which totaled more than 476 million pounds in 1991. Included in that total were 58 million pounds of pesticides that were not registered or had been banned, suspended, or restricted for use in the United States. These hazardous products "were exported at a rate of nearly 80 tons per day . . . an increase over the rate of 72 tons per day noted by Foundation researchers in 1990. More than half of these products were shipped to developing countries, where unsafe storage and application practices are common."[2]

Many of the compounds exported are "known or suspected to cause cancer, mutagenesis (genetic mutation), and adverse prenatal or reproductive effects," FASE reported. One of the extremely hazardous pesticides exported was paraquat. Out of a total 9.3 million pounds shipped, more than 1.7 million pounds of paraquat went to rural Guatemala. "Based on estimates of the dose sufficient to cause severe paraquat poisoning [which leads to death within twenty-four hours after ingestion] . . . this quantity of paraquat is enough to fatally poison each inhabitant of rural Guatemala nearly thirty-five times," FASE reported.

Many of the total pesticides exported are identified only by generic names such as "weed killer," by trade names, or by the name of their chemical family. Thus FASE has consistently argued in reports and in testimony before the U.S. Congress that complete information about pesticide exports "should be a matter of public record" and that receiving countries should be informed about the legal status, content, and safe use of imported pesticides. The practice of exporting banned pesticides is "disgraceful," FASE stated, concluding that U.S. export practices "contribute significantly to the likelihood of extensive health and environmental damage" in the United States and abroad.[3]

Some attempts have been made to ban unsafe pesticide exports. President Jimmy Carter, for example, issued an executive order in 1981 banning the export of toxic pesticides and other hazardous products. But President Ronald Reagan revoked that order when he took office, and the policy of exporting hazardous pesticides remained in force throughout his two terms and also throughout the administration of President George Bush.

Since 1990, legislation known as COPPA—the Circle of Poison Prevention Act—has been introduced and reintroduced in the U.S. Congress. Even though the proposed law has had wide support in both houses of Congress, including cosponsorship of the bill by former senator Albert Gore, members have yet to vote on the legislation. Still, supporters hope that Vice President Gore, who has long condemned hazardous dumping and other threats to the environment, will press for passage of COPPA, which would prohibit or limit the export of U.S.-banned pesticides.

Even though COPPA has not yet become law, the EPA has made some changes in its policies on pesticide exports. In February 1993, the agency released new regulations that require U.S. companies to notify importing nations of potential hazards of pesticides being exported. "The new policy is a major step towards improved information exchange," according to Sandra Marquardt of Greenpeace's toxic trade campaign. But, she added, "notification is not enough when it comes down to the export of banned and never registered pesticides. Along with hundreds of other groups, Greenpeace believes that EPA should adopt a complete ban on the export of unregistered pesticides, enforce stronger restrictions on the export of highly hazardous pesticides, and disseminate information on nonchemical alternatives to pesticides."[4]

TRADE IN TOXIC WASTE

Along with calling attention to hazardous pesticide exports from the United States, many environmental and civil rights groups also have focused on international trade in toxic waste. Such trade was hardly a problem until the 1980s. As U.S. regulations strengthened to prevent uncontrolled dumping of hazardous wastes, American industries, disposal companies, and government agencies sought ways to get rid of dangerous materials. One of those methods was to ship toxic wastes out of the country, as a 1990 public television documentary, "Global Dumping Ground," graphically illustrated.

Toxic waste exports from the United States to other countries have been documented in news stories published over the past decade. And Greenpeace, an international environmental organization that began a campaign in 1987 to ban toxic waste exports, issued a massive inventory in

100

1990 of waste trade exports from numerous countries world-wide. Greenpeace workers were able to document at least one thousand incidents of trade in toxic waste by photographing actual dumping, by researching shipping reports and court records, and by interviewing waste traders and importers.

Some U.S. shipments have included exports of toxic wastes labeled "recyclable" or "recycled" so that they can be dumped in other countries. In other instances, hazardous wastes have been mixed with fertilizers for export overseas. Sometimes drums of toxic waste have been illegally transported by truck across the U.S.-Canadian and the U.S.-Mexican borders and dumped at unregulated sites.

A few U.S. laws and an international treaty called the Basel Convention—signed in 1989 and named for Basel, Switzerland, where the first international meetings on transboundary shipments of toxic waste were held—are supposed to regulate trade in toxic waste. But there is little real control over toxic trade worldwide. In fact, activists say that many governments, including the administrations of former presidents Ronald Reagan and George Bush, have encouraged toxic waste exports. In the words of Greenpeace organizers: "The Reagan-Bush era left a legacy of toxic waste dumping on every continent, from farms in Bangladesh, to a beach in Haiti, to the edge of a South African 'homeland.' "[5]

Activists also cite an infamous example of support for toxic dumping on poor countries, which came from the World Bank, the international lending institution. Its chief economist, Lawrence Summers, advised in an internal memo—leaked to the press and published in magazines and newspapers worldwide in February 1992—that the World Bank should "be encouraging more migration of dirty industries to LDCs [less developed countries]. Health-impairing pollution should be done in the country with the lowest cost, which will also be the country with the lowest wages. I think the economic logic behind dumping a load of toxic waste in the lowest wage country is impeccable and we should face up to that."[6]

101

Environmentalists and civil rights activists were outraged over Summers's apparent lack of concern for human health hazards. On the other hand, "many economists favored easing environmental restraints on Third World industries in order to encourage growth," according to a report in *Facts on File*, which also included Summers's claim that his "memo was an ironic piece intended to stimulate debate on global economic issues."[7]

A *Boston Globe* editorial agreed that "there is some logic to the notion that economic growth, even 'dirty' economic growth, is probably preferable to poverty, which is a greater cause of suffering in the Third World than the presence of power plants and landfills." The editorial noted that if there is going to be a trade-off between a cleaner environment and less poverty, then most poor countries would probably tolerate more pollution than rich countries would. But the editorial clearly disagreed with that kind of justification, stating that the argument "has been made for years in [the United States] that poor communities will welcome the tax revenues and jobs (even if they are low-paying) that the siting of dirty industries would bring. Might it be possible that poor communities would welcome even more the siting of clean industries and the fullest range of . . . protections?" the editorial asked.[8]

EXPLOITATION SOUTH OF THE BORDER

Such a question is often posed in regard to dumping toxic waste and siting dirty industries south of the U.S. border. Large quantities of hazardous materials generated by U.S. companies are illegally sent to Mexico for disposal. Although U.S. companies contract with waste haulers to take industrial waste to legal disposal sites in the United States, the haulers may disguise hazardous waste by combining it with bulk trash loaded onto railroad cars or by filling barrels piled onto trucks for shipment to Mexico. Haulers then dump toxic trash in remote areas or store barrels of hazardous waste in abandoned warehouses. These practices continue because the Mexican environmental agency, called SEDUE, does not have the funds or the staff to adequately monitor and control illegal toxic dumping.

A more widely publicized disposal problem is the hazardous waste coming from industries that corporations based in the United States, Japan, and other countries have built along the border between the United States and Mexico. Under an economic development plan, the Mexican government offered companies incentives, such as a cheap labor force and low taxes, to locate in Mexico. About two thousand companies, the majority of which are U.S.-owned, took advantage of the plan and built factories, primarily assembly plants. Assembled products are then returned to twin plants (*maquilas*) in the United States where the products are packaged.

However, in this *maquiladora* system, as it is called, there is little similarity between the packaging plants and the assembly plants. Even if U.S. workers earn only minimum wage, their income is much greater than that of Mexican workers who do most of the labor and earn an average of $27 a week. Mexican workers have few protections from workplace hazards such as exposure to radioactive materials and toxic chemicals. Joseph LaDou, medical director of the International Commission on Occupational Health, has investigated working conditions in many newly industrialized nations, including Mexico. He reported that in the Mexican border towns "Many owners and managers—especially of small *maquiladoras* engaged in metal working, plating, printing, tanning, and dyeing—readily admit that they moved their operations to Mexico partly because hazardous processes are unwelcome in the United States and other developed countries."[9]

Workers frequently are exposed to toxins used in the assembly plants and other *maquiladora* industries. In the town of Matamoros, for example, a former U.S. company, Mallory Capacitors, hired women to work with highly toxic PCBs. "The women often had to reach into deep vats of PCBs with no protection other than rubber gloves. Many

103

of the workers developed the chloracne rash these chemicals typically cause," LaDou reported. He also noted that at least twenty children whose mothers worked with PCBs were born mentally retarded.[10]

Hazardous wastes from border industries also endanger the health of workers' families who live nearby. Toxic materials contaminate water supplies and land areas, and dangerous emissions pollute the air. U.S. companies insist that they are complying with an agreement between the Mexican and U.S. governments, which requires that hazardous waste be sent from assembly plants to the United States for treatment. However, reports from investigators have shown just the opposite to be true. Levels of some hazardous materials dumped into the environment are thousands of times higher than would be allowed in the United States.[11]

Some efforts are under way to bring about environmental justice for workers in the *maquiladora* system. In 1991, for example, more than sixty environmental, religious, and labor organizations formed the Coalition for Justice in the Maquiladoras. Sister Susan Mika, a coalition board member and president of the Benedictine Sisters working in the border city of San Antonio, Texas, announced that the coalition was "a binational alliance which seeks to pressure transnational corporations to adopt socially responsible practices within the *maquiladora* industry."

During a press conference at the coalition headquarters in New York City, Sister Susan Mika called on corporations to contribute more to border cities such as Ciudad Juárez, where many U.S. plants are located. "When compared to U.S. operations, corporations save $25,000 a year per worker in their *maquiladora* operations. With over 135,000 workers in Juárez alone, the corporations are saving more than $3 billion a year in labor costs," she noted in her formal statement, adding, "We are not asking the corporations to forgo all of these savings. But we are convinced that they can afford to do much more to improve the quality of life on both sides of the border."[12]

9
SEEKING ENVIRONMENTAL JUSTICE

Over the past few years, many more individuals and groups have been demanding improvements in the quality of their environment and thus their lives, with the issue of environmental justice gaining many new advocates. In fact, the growing multicultural, multiracial movement against environmental racism and for environmental justice has prompted action on many fronts, including support for federal and state legislation that seeks to bring about environmental equity.

FEDERAL LEGISLATIVE ACTIONS

In 1992, then Senator Al Gore and U.S. Representative John Lewis of Georgia cosponsored a bill proposing an Environmental Justice Act, which would ensure equal protection from environmental hazards and enforcement of environmental laws without discrimination. Although the bill did not pass, Congressman Lewis again submitted the proposed law in May 1993. A similar bill was introduced in the Senate a month later.

The Environmental Justice Act is expected to include provisions requiring that data be collected to identify the one hundred worst counties in the United States where people are exposed to excessive amounts of toxic substances. It also would provide funds for programs aimed at reducing health risks from environmental hazards. One of the main goals of the proposed law is to empower citizens threatened by multiple sources of pollution. The act provides mechanisms to enable citizens to intervene in decisions such as where hazardous waste dumps or incinerators will be located.

Civil rights laws passed years ago were used in the fall of 1993 as a basis for filing the first "environmental justice" complaints with the EPA. The suits against the states of Mississippi and Louisiana were filed by the Sierra Club's Legal Defense Fund on behalf of residents, alleging that the states had discriminated against people of color by locating hazardous waste facilities in their communities, violating the Civil Rights Act of 1964.

Other proposed federal laws may also help reduce inequities in exposure to toxic pollutants. One is the Community Right to Know More Act, which in effect expands the Community Right to Know Act of 1986. Under the 1986 law, industries must report to the EPA the amount of toxic chemicals they release into the environment. The Right to Know More Act would increase the number of toxic chemicals beyond the three hundred or so that must be reported at present.

The U.S. Congress also may reauthorize the RCRA (the Resource Conservation and Recovery Act), the principal federal law regulating solid and hazardous waste. No funds have been allocated to implement the act since late 1988, although the EPA receives federal funds to continue RCRA programs and to enforce RCRA regulations.

If RCRA is reauthorized, which is not expected to happen until 1995, Congress probably will amend the law to address a variety of waste disposal issues such as ensuring

Grassroots groups have organized referendums as a means of fighting back. Ninety-three percent of the votes cast in this election were against the incinerator.

safer landfills and incinerators, developing recycling facilities, and establishing requirements to reduce waste at the source. Dozens of amendments to RCRA proposed laws to deal with hazardous and solid waste have been introduced already. Most of these aim to reduce garbage and hazardous waste by stimulating recycling through tax incentives, grants, deposit-refund systems, requirements for use of recycled materials in packaging, and other mechanisms.

In early 1994, Congress passed legislation elevating the EPA to the Department of Environmental Protection, with the head of the department becoming a member of the president's cabinet. The department will include a Bureau of Environmental Statistics, which will compile and analyze statistics on environmental quality and will publish an annual report showing the amounts of various pollutants and how they affect public health and the environment. Among other responsibilities, the new department also will help small businesses and local governments comply with environmental regulations, establish measures to protect Native American lands, and help ensure equity in environmental programs. When the new department is fully established in 1994, it will also provide the means for the United States to take a stronger leadership role in solving global environmental problems.

STATE ACTIONS

A few states also have passed laws that promote environmental equity. In Georgia, for example, legislators have proposed a state Environmental Justice Act. This legislation, if it passes, will require the state to identify the communities that suffer the highest levels of pollution and prevent any further environmental contamination of those areas. Another provision of the bill will require local governments to hold public hearings before contracting to site any waste disposal facility or polluting industry.

In Tennessee, the state legislature passed a law in 1991 that provided the legal mechanism to set up an environmental court. Such a court deals with people arrested for violating local codes designed to protect public health and safety. In most other states, such cases are usually heard in criminal courts, and because the courts are crowded with many misdemeanor cases, the environmental cases receive scant attention; violators may be dismissed with small fines or only warnings. An environmental court, on the other hand, has the power to prosecute polluters and impose fines and jail sentences for violating environmental and health protection laws.

Dozens of other states that do not have specific laws addressing environmental injustices have at least passed legislation or proposed bills that deal with these issues, particularly waste disposal and emissions. Legislation is designed to prevent or reduce the amount of toxic waste or emissions at their source rather than try to clean up or treat poisonous materials after they are produced. For example, a few states have prohibited the construction of waste incinerators until toxic waste is reduced. The Indiana General Assembly has been considering a Market Development Bill, which would ban disposal of recyclable materials in landfills and incinerators and would promote the development of markets for recyclables. Minnesota passed a pollution prevention law that includes funding for a Community Assistance Program to support community-based projects emphasizing cooperation between business owners and citizens to reduce pollutants at the source. One proposed project in Saint Paul would include representatives from business and civic groups and university students, who would work in eco-teams to identify and try to prevent pollution.

REDUCING TOXIC MATERIALS
AND WASTE

Despite the laws and regulations passed at local, state, and federal levels to reduce the amount of toxic waste and emissions at their source, the volume of poisonous materials entering the environment and endangering people is still huge. In May 1993, the EPA released a report showing that 24,000 of the 200,000 U.S. industries that manufacture or use chemicals generated 38 billion pounds of waste in 1991. EPA administrator Carol Browner called such a huge volume of waste "the equivalent of a line of tank trucks that stretches halfway around the world."[1]

Some manufacturing companies and business corporations are beginning to decrease or eliminate the toxicity of the materials used in their industrial or business operations. One well-publicized example is the McDonald's Corporation, which, after several years of protests by environmental activists, has cut its solid-waste output by one half since 1991 and has switched to recycled packaging materials.

Industrial firms can take some relatively simple steps to bring about a 90 percent reduction in the total waste stream of the nation. By doing so, companies can save $3.50 annually for each dollar spent, according to INFORM, a non-profit research organization that publishes information to help citizens find practical solutions to waste-related and other pollution problems. In 1993, INFORM published *Preventing Industrial Toxic Hazards*, a guide designed to help grassroots groups cooperate with local industrial plants to reduce toxic chemicals at the source. Citizens first need to know what types of industry are located in their communities, and much of that information is available from public sources, which are listed in the guide. The publication also shows how a source reduction program works and how it differs from managing or controlling waste after it is produced. In addition, the guide explains how to contact company officials, set up interviews with plant representatives, and create an atmosphere that will help bring about a good-neighbor policy on the part of corporations.

One such effort was successful in Austin, Texas, where a research group sponsored by the federal government and industry is located. Called the Semiconductor Manufacturing Technology Initiative (SEMATECH), the group represents eleven major semiconductor manufacturers, including

AT&T, Hewlett Packard, IBM, and Intel. The alliance was formed in 1987 to reduce U.S. dependence on foreign companies as sources for computer microchips, which the U.S. Department of Defense said jeopardized national security, since high-technology computers are essential to many military operations. Member companies contribute to research efforts, and their contributions are matched by the Department of Defense.

But there is no government mandate to find ways to prevent toxic pollution of the environment and workplace, which has been a concern of many citizens working in or living near computer manufacturing companies. In 1991, two citizen groups, the Campaign for Responsible Technology and the Southwest Network for Environmental and Economic Justice, tried to persuade the research group to broaden its mission from developing the most advanced computer technology to also devising cleaner and safer technologies for the computer industry. But SEMATECH said such a mission was beyond its scope. So the two citizen groups conducted a campaign that persuaded Congress to pass regulations in 1992, requiring SEMATECH to spend 10 percent of its $100 million budget on research into alternative clean production technologies. "Congress also mandated that SEMATECH work with labor and environmental groups in deciding how that $10 million should be spent," according to a report from Environmental Exchange, a Washington, D.C., organization that issues a monthly bulletin on successful environmental projects.[2]

Some companies are preventing pollution by recovering toxic materials on site and reusing them rather than allowing them to be released into the environment. Hoffmann-La Roche in New Jersey, for instance, has been able to prevent the release of toxic gases from solvents (cleaners) and recover solvents with the use of steam strippers. In the process solvents are vaporized and condensed and recycled back into the manufacturing process. Another New Jersey-based company, AT&T, has developed a variety of new cleaning technologies that eliminate the use of hazardous solvents; one makes use of a natural cleaner derived from oranges. The company also has developed solder pastes made from food ingredients that dissolve in water.

Another way companies are reducing toxic materials is through the use of recycled raw materials and packaging. While environmentalists have long called for more use of recyclables in business and industry as a way to reduce toxins, companies have only recently begun to respond. An alliance of twenty-five major corporations, including Sears Roebuck and Du Pont, announced in 1992 that they had created a program to increase the use of recycled products, urging their suppliers to provide recycled raw materials as well as manufactured goods, such as packaging, made with recycled material. The use of recycled goods is expected to save companies millions of dollars each year. Sears, for example, projected a savings of $5 million annually.[3]

The computer industry appears to be at the forefront in developing ways not only to recycle but also to prevent pollution at the manufacturing end. According to a report in the New York Times, 10 million computers are being discarded annually, and at that rate "some 150 million computer carcasses will reside in the nation's landfills by the year 2005," which could cost up to $1 billion for disposal alone and create a serious environmental problem.[4]

Business and government are working together in a model program called Design for Environment that is attempting to develop manufacturing processes that make use of recyclable materials. In the computer industry this means making changes in computer designs so that discarded machines can be dismantled easily for recycling. One New Jersey company, Advanced Recovery, already takes scrap computers apart to recover various metals, such as aluminum and gold. Efforts are under way in other companies to melt down plastic housings and parts from discarded computers and combine them with new plastic resins to make plastic frameworks for new machines. Still another method of preventing pollution from cast-off computers is to collect and ship them to organizations, schools, and other institutions, particularly in developing countries, where they can be used.

LONG-TERM GOALS

There is still a long way to go before the vast amount of contaminants in the environment is reduced nationwide, particularly in communities that have been neglected or deliberately dumped on. One of the first steps toward eliminating environmental hazards in vulnerable communities is educating the public about the problem.

That educational process takes many forms, such as magazine and newspaper articles, books, and other published materials that describe and explain environmental justice issues. Television documentaries and networks of activists communicating by computer also help spread the word.

Public events such as conferences and fund-raisers help educate the general public as well. One event, called "A Night of Solidarity with the People of Kettleman City and Bay Area Communities of Color Fighting Environmental Racism," was held in San Francisco in March 1993; it called attention to four environmental justice groups in California. One of the groups was El Pueblo para Aire y Agua Limpio (People for Clean Air and Water), which had been fighting for years to stop construction of a hazardous waste facility in Kettleman City. Six months after the event, the group could finally claim victory: Chemical Waste Management discarded its plan to build a giant incinerator in Kettleman City.

Another group highlighted at the San Francisco event has been conducting a multilingual program to educate people about childhood lead poisoning; a third has been fighting Chevron and other oil companies that have been polluting their neighborhoods for many years.

A fourth group worked to defeat a state government effort to rebuild a freeway in West Oakland that was destroyed in a 1989 earthquake. A coalition of people from this community of 7,000, which is 75 percent African

American, 9 percent Asian, and 8 percent Latino, filed a lawsuit against the state, charging that rebuilding the freeway would cause damage to the health and environment of the community. The suit also claimed that the state did not consider other alternatives that would be less costly, but instead wanted to rebuild where politicians assumed there would be the least resistance. According to the leader of the coalition, Chappell Hayes, the lawsuit was filed "in the same tradition that people of color have sought redress in the courts for discrimination in housing and employment." The suit pointed to "discrimination in our environment," Hayes said. He went on to explain:

> Everybody wants pretty much the same thing in basic terms, and that's respect and consideration. If we were given that in adequate measure, organizing would be very difficult. But since we are so patently denied, we just present ourselves and give people an opportunity to weigh in what's going on. Together, we fashion sometimes the most simple strategies like protest[ing], and that helps us focus our complaints. Or sometimes we do voter registration. We know that some politicians who represent us are very sorry. They need to be aired and replaced every once in a while, so we try to arm the community in that way. Finally, as a last resort, we recognize as many of our constitutional rights as we can, and we assert them to the greatest extent possible.[5]

Many people on the front line fighting for environmental justice take actions similar to those of the West Oakland group. They also focus on broad goals, which was evident at the 1993 convention of the Grassroots Movement for Environmental Justice. Delegates cited dozens of aims that they hoped to achieve. Those aims included the following:

• Uniting and organizing in environmental justice causes, people who previously have been separated because of racial, ethnic, religious, class, age, language, or geographical differences.

- Working for community participation and control in the way public policies are made in regard to pollution prevention.
- Promoting choices of consumer goods and lifestyles that are environmentally sound—that is, do not contribute to toxic emissions, hazardous waste, or destruction of the environment.
- Supporting workers' efforts to reduce toxins in the workplace.
- Educating the public on waste disposal problems and the need for citizen participation in determining where waste disposal sites and dirty industries will be located.
- Demanding that elected government officials be accountable to all their constituents, not just to the politically powerful, and that government agencies carry out their mission to protect citizens, regardless of their economic or ethnic background, from environmental hazards.
- Guarding against the development of additional national "sacrifice zones," such as Louisiana's petrochemical corridor and Altgeld Gardens in Chicago.

Many other action plans and aims have been outlined. But one of the leading promoters of environmental justice has perhaps best summarized the basic long-term goal of the movement. In the words of Benjamin Chavis: "Environmental justice advocates are not saying, 'Take the poisons out of our community and put them in a white community.' They are saying that no community should have to live with these poisons. They have thus taken the moral high road and are building a multiracial and inclusive movement that has the potential of transforming the political landscape of this nation."[6]

SOURCE NOTES

Chapter 1

1. "Home Street, USA: Living with Pollution," *Greenpeace*, October, November, December 1991, 3.
2. Robert F. Kennedy, Jr., and Dennis Rivera, "Pollution's Chief Victims: The Poor," *New York Times*, August 15, 1992, 19.
3. Roberto Suro, "Pollution-Weary Minorities Try Civil Rights Tack," *New York Times*, January 11, 1993, A1.
4. Robert D. Bullard, "Environmental Racism," transcript of an address delivered at the University of Colorado at Boulder, February 4, 1992.
5. Ibid.
6. Dollie Burwell, "Reminiscences from Warren County, North Carolina," in Charles Lee, ed., *Proceedings of the First National People of Color Environmental Leadership Summit*, October 24–27, 1991 (New York: United Church of Christ Commission for Racial Justice, 1992), 126.
7. Quoted in Karl Grossman, "From Toxic Racism to Environmental Justice," *E* Magazine, May-June 1992, 31.

8. Bunyan Bryant and Paul Mohai, "The Michigan Conference: A Turning Point," *EPA Journal*, March-April 1992, 9–10.

9. Quoted in Michael Weisskopf, "Rights Group Finds Racism in Dump Siting," *Washington Post*, April 16, 1987, A7.

10. Linda-Jo Schierow, "Environmental Equity," *CRS Report for Congress*, August 14, 1992, 5.

11. Charles Lee, ed., *Proceedings of the First National People of Color Environmental Leadership Summit*, October 24–27, 1991 (New York: United Church of Christ Commission for Racial Justice, 1992), *v*.

Chapter 2

1. Charles Jordan and Donald Snow, "Diversification, Minorities, and the Mainstream Environmental Movement," in Donald Snow, ed., *Voices from the Environmental Movement* (Washington, D.C.: Conservation Fund, 1992), 75–79.

2. Quoted in Marcia Davis, "Audubon Broadens Sights," *Washington Post*, January 7, 1993, J7.

3. Robert D. Bullard, "Anatomy of Environmental Racism and the Environmental Justice Movement," in Robert D. Bullard, ed., *Confronting Environmental Racism: Voices from the Grassroots* (Boston: South End Press, 1993), 23.

4. Robert F. Kennedy Jr. and Dennis Rivera, "Pollution's Chief Victims: The Poor," *New York Times*, August 15, 1992, 19.

5. Quoted in Scott Bronstein, "Are Poor Rural Blacks Targets of Waste Facility Site Decisions?" *Atlanta Constitution*, February 22, 1993, A1.

6. Ibid.

7. Ibid.

8. Donald G. Schueler, "Southern Exposure," *Sierra*, November-December 1992, 46.

9. Special Investigation Report (insert), *National Law Journal*, September 14, 1992, 2.

10. Ibid.

11. Claudia MacLachlan (special insert, community profile), "Unto the Third Generation," *National Law Journal*, September 21, 1992, 11.

12. MacLachlan, p. 7.

13. Quoted in Michael Weisskopf, "Minorities' Pollution Risk Is Debated," *Washington Post*, January 16, 1992, A25.

14. Quoted in Michael Weisskopf, "EPA's Two Voices on Pollution Risks to Minorities," *Washington Post*, March 9, 1992, A15.

15. Ibid.

Chapter 3

1. Janet Phoenix, "Getting the Lead Out of the Community," in Robert D. Bullard, ed., *Confronting Environmental Racism: Voices from the Grassroots* (Boston: South End Press, 1993), 78.

2. Quoted in "Government Steps Up Efforts to Prevent Lead Poisoning," *Chemecology*, February 1991, 10.

3. Sally Squires, "The Cutting Edge—Lead Poisoning Tests Not for All Children?" *Washington Post*, June 1, 1993, Z5.

4. Statistical sidebar in Steven Waldman, "Lead and Your Kids," *Newsweek*, July 15, 1991, 43.

5. "Is There Lead in Your Water?" *Consumer Reports*, February 1993, 73–78.

6. "Forty Years of Environmental Racism," *RACHEL'S Hazardous Waste News*, weekly newsletter from the Environmental Research Foundation, July 15, 1992.

7. "Let Them Eat Lead," *Washington Post*, February 10, 1973, A14.

8. Marianne C. Fahs, "White House Should Stay with Lead Cleanup," *New York Times*, September 18, 1991, A18.

9. Philip J. Hilts, "White House Shuns Key Role in Lead Exposure," *New York Times*, August 24, 1991, 14.

10. Quoted in "Old Paint May Be Biggest Culprit," *Columbus Dispatch*, January 10, 1983, 4G.

11. Michael Weitzman, Ann Aschengrau, David Bellinger,

Ronald Jones, Julie Shea Hamlin, and Alexa Beiser, "Lead-Contaminated Soil Abatement and Urban Children's Blood Lead Levels," *Journal of the American Medical Association,* April 7, 1993, abstract, 1647.

Chapter 4

1. Keith Schneider, "Panel Finds No Wide Threat of Cancer Caused by Dioxin," *New York Times,* September 26, 1992, 9.
2. Rose Gatfeld, "Dioxin's Health Risks May Be Greater Than Believed," *Wall Street Journal,* October 16, 1992, B9.
3. Jeff Bailey, "Dueling Studies: How Two Industries Created a Fresh Spin on the Dioxin Debate," *Wall Street Journal,* February 20, 1992, A1.
4. Keith Schneider, "What Price Cleanup?" (series) *New York Times,* March 21–24, March 26, 1993.
5. Quoted in Don Hopey, "Incinerator Health, Safety Issues Fuel Heated Debate," *Pittsburgh Press,* March 15, 1992, A1.
6. Quoted in Denise Kearns, "Incineration: A Burning Issue," *Chemecology,* March 1993, 15.
7. Hopey, "Incinerator Health," A1.
8. Quoted in Roberto Suro, "Environmental, Civil Rights Forces Join Up," *Oregonian,* January 13, 1993, A3.
9. Billy Easgon, "WHE ACT for Justice," *Environmental Action,* Winter 1993, 34.
10. Quoted in Ginny Carroll, "When Pollution Hits Home," *National Wildlife,* August-September 1991, 36.
11. Pat Bryant, "A View from Down Below" in Charles Lee, ed., *Proceedings of the First National People of Color Environmental Leadership Summit, October 24–27, 1991* (New York: United Church of Christ Commission for Racial Justice, 1991), 84–85.

Chapter 5

1. Quoted in Dick Russell, "Dances With Waste," *Amicus Journal,* Fall 1991, 28–29.

2. Thomas A. Daschle, "Dances With Garbage," *Christian Science Monitor,* February 14, 1991, 18; Paul Schneider, "Other People's Trash," *Audubon,* July-August, 1991, 108–19; Mary Hager with Bill Harlan, Michael Mason, and Andrew Murr, " 'Dances With Garbage,' " *Newsweek,* April 29, 1991, 36.

3. Peter Montague, " 'Hush-Hush' at Huerfano Mountain—Government Permits Another Time Bomb," *RACHEL'S Hazardous Waste News,* March 25, 1992.

4. "Racism and Nuclear Power," electronic news release, ACT for Disarmament, EcoNet, May 19, 1993.

5. Keith Schneider, "A Valley of Death for the Navajo Uranium Miners," *New York Times,* May 3, 1993, A1.

6. Schneider, A8.

7. Charles Laszewski, "Prairie Island's Pool of Trouble," *Saint Paul Pioneer Press,* January 31, 1993, 16A.

8. Quoted in Prairie Island Tribal Council press release, "Minnesota Indian Reservation Applies for Consideration as Federal High-Level Nuclear Waste Facility," January 9, 1992.

9. Charles Laszewski, "Indian Leaders Vote to End Atomic Waste Storage Study," *Saint Paul Pioneer Press,* June 11, 1993, 2C; Laszewski, "NSP to Appeal Nuclear Waste Decision," *Saint Paul Pioneer Press,* June 9, 1993, 1A; related stories in the *Saint Paul Pioneer Press,* June 6 and June 8, 1993.

Chapter 6

1. "NRDC Report Calls for Pesticide Phase Outs and Overhaul of Pesticide Laws," Pesticide Action Network North America Updates Service, electronic news release, EcoNet, June 24, 1993.

2. "Two Reports on Food Safety," Pesticide Action Network North America Updates Service, electronic news release, EcoNet, July 6, 1993.

3. Quoted in Marian Burros, "U.S. Is Taking Aim at Farm

Chemicals in the Food Supply," *New York Times,* June 27, 1993, A1.

4. Bill Lambrecht, "Groups Urge Ban on Some Pesticides," *Saint Louis Post Dispatch,* June 22, 1993, 1C.

5. Quoted in Penny Newman and Hubert Dixon III, "Chemical Warfare in America: The Plague of Pesticides," *Everyone's Backyard,* October 1991, 5.

6. Quoted in "Insecticides on Native Land," Pesticide Action Network North America Updates Service, electronic news release, EcoNet, July 3, 1992.

7. Ibid.

8. Marion Moses, "Farmworkers and Pesticides," in Robert D. Bullard, ed., *Confronting Environmental Racism* (Boston: South End Press, 1993), 161.

9. Moses, 163.

10. Moses, 162–65.

11. *Los Angeles Times* news service, " 'Grapes of Wrath' Return for Many Farmworkers," *Seattle Times,* April 28, 1993, A3.

12. George Rede and the Associated Press, "Report Exposes 'Alarming' Plight of Migrants," *Oregonian,* February 25, 1992, B4.

13. Maria Dolan, "EPA Asks U.S. to Ban Pesticide," *Los Angeles Times,* March 27, 1991, B1.

14. Quoted in "Spraying of Migrant Workers Probed," *Atlanta Constitution,* June 13, 1992, B10.

15. Quoted in "Florida Farmworkers to Protest at the Regional EPA in Atlanta," Farmworker Association of Central Florida press release, November 4, 1992.

16. "Farmworkers Get Grant to Study Pesticide Exposure," *Oregonian,* July 21, 1992, Foodday Section, 3.

17. "U.S. Begins Long-Term Study of Farm Family Health," Pesticide Action Network North America press release, March 12, 1993.

18. Kathlyn Gay, *Cleaning Nature Naturally* (New York: Walker, 1991), 9–15.

Chapter 7

1. Quoted in "Action Line," *Everyone's Backyard,* June 1992, 19.
2. George F. Will, "Chicken Littles: The Persistence of Eco-Pessimism," *Washington Post,* May 31, 1992, C7.
3. Gary Benoit, "Letter from the Editor," *New American,* June 1, 1992, 3.
4. " 'Wise Use' Revisited," *RACHEL'S Hazardous Waste News,* April 29, 1993.
5. Richard M. Stapleton, "Greed vs. Green," *National Parks,* November-December 1992, 32–37; William Poole, "Neither Wise Nor Well," *Sierra,* November-December 1992, 59–61 and 88–93.
6. Quoted in Colman McCarthy, "Earth and the Religious Challenge," *Washington Post,* June 2, 1992, D19.
7. Kevin Lynch and Rebecca Rosen, "The 'Wise Use' Movement Declares War," *Greenpeace,* January-February-March 1991, 10–11.
8. Quoted in " 'Wise Use' Revisited," *RACHEL'S Hazardous Waste News,* April 29, 1993.
9. Quoted in Will Nixon, "Fear and Loathing in the Adirondacks," *E Magazine,* September-October 1992, 31.
10. Nixon, 35.
11. Quoted in Catherine Dold, "SLAPP Back!" *Buzzworm: The Environmental Journal,* July-August 1992, 36.
12. Quoted in "Incinerator Opponent Wins Damages," *BNA California Environment Daily,* October 29, 1992.
13. Ibid.

Chapter 8

1. "Exporting Banned and Hazardous Pesticides, 1991 Statistics," Special Supplement, FASE Reports, Spring 1993, S1.
2. Ibid.
3. FASE Reports, S3–S8.
4. Sandra Marquardt, "U.S. Defines New Pesticides Exports

Policy," *Greenpeace Toxic Trade Update 6.1*, First Quarter 1993, 7.

5. "A Fresh Start to the U.S. Toxic Trade Debate," *Greenpeace Toxic Trade Update 6.1*, First Quarter 1993, 6.

6. Quoted in "Global Environment: World Bank Memo Sparks Furor," *Facts on File*, March 12, 1992, 162D3.

7. Ibid. Also, Michael Weisskopf, "World Bank Official's Irony Backfires," *Washington Post*, February 10, 1992, A9.

8. "Environmental Equity," editorial, *Boston Globe*, February 26, 1992, 12.

9. Joseph LaDou, "Deadly Migration," *Technology Review*, July 1991, 50.

10. LaDou, 52.

11. Kathlyn Gay, *Global Garbage: Exporting Trash and Toxic Waste* (New York: Franklin Watts, 1992), 36–40.

12. Sister Susan Mika, Coalition for Justice in the Maquiladoras, press conference, New York City, February 12, 1991.

Chapter 9

1. "INFORM Guide Empowers Citizens to Spur Local Industries to Slash Toxic Chemical Waste in Their Communities," INFORM electronic news release, June 18, 1993.

2. "Activists Shape High-Tech Research Priorities," Environmental Exchange Bulletin, electronic news release, Eco-Net, July 19, 1993.

3. Frank O'Donnell, "Corporate America Turns on to the Environment," *Nature Conservancy*, January-February 1993, 31.

4. Steve Lohr, "Recycling Answer Sought for Computer Junk," *New York Times*, April 14, 1993, A1.

5. Quoted in Penn Loh, "Freeways, Communities, and Environmental Justice," New Liberation News Service electronic news service, August 7, 1993.

6. Benjamin F. Chavis Jr., Foreword, in Robert D. Bullard, ed., *Confronting Environmental Racism: Voices from the Grassroots* (Boston: South End Press, 1993), 5.

FOR FURTHER READING

Books

Alston, Danna. *We Speak for Ourselves: Social Justice, Race, and Environment.* Washington, D.C.: The Panos Institute, 1990.

Angel, Bradley. *The Toxic Threat to Indian Lands: A Greenpeace Report.* San Francisco: Greenpeace, 1992.

Bullard, Robert D. *Dumping in Dixie: Race, Class, and Environmental Quality.* Boulder, CO: Westview Press, 1990.

Bullard, Robert D., ed. *Confronting Environmental Racism: Voices from the Grassroots.* Boston: South End Press, 1993.

Center for Investigative Reporting and Bill Moyers. *Global Dumping Ground: International Traffic in Hazardous Waste.* Washington, D.C.: Seven Locks Press, 1990.

Gay, Kathlyn. *Global Garbage: Exporting Trash and Toxic Waste.* New York: Franklin Watts, 1992.

Gore, Al. *Earth in the Balance: Ecology and the Human Spirit.* New York: Plume/Penguin Books, 1993.

Lee, Charles, ed. *The First National People of Color Environmental Leadership Summit.* New York: United Church of Christ, 1992.

Snow, Donald, ed. *Voices from the Environmental Movement.* Washington, D.C.: The Conservation Fund, 1992.

United Church of Christ Commission for Racial Justice. *Toxic Wastes and Race in the United States.* New York: United Church of Christ, 1987.

Urrea, Luis Alberto. *Across the Wire: Life and Hard Times on the Mexican Border.* New York: Anchor Books, 1993.

Vallette, Jim, and Heather Spalding. *The International Trade in Wastes: A Greenpeace Inventory.* Washington, D.C.: Greenpeace U.S.A., 1990.

Weir, David, and Mark Schapiro. *Circle of Poison.* San Francisco: Institute for Food and Development Policy, 1981.

Magazine Articles

Angel, Bradley. "Beyond White Environmentalism." *Environmental Action,* January/February 1990, 19–30.

Carroll, Ginny. "When Pollution Hits Home." *National Wildlife,* August/September 1991, 30–40.

Dowie, Mark. "The New Face of Environmentalism." *Utne Reader,* July/August 1992, 104–11.

Grossman, Karl. "From Toxic Racism to Environmental Justice." *E Magazine,* May/June 1992, 28–35.

"Home Street U.S.A.: People Living with Pollution." *Greenpeace,* October/November/December 1991, 8–13.

Lapp, David. "Fighting for the Right to Breathe Free." (Interview with Jesse Jackson). *E Magazine,* May/June 1992, 10–13.

Margolis, Mark, with Mac Margolis. "The Fate of the Earth." *Maclean's,* December 16, 1991, 32–36.

"Poverty, Population, Pollution." *Unesco,* January 1992, 18–21.

Schneider, Paul. "Other People's Trash." *Audubon,* July/August 1991, 109–119.

Schueler, Donald G. "Southern Exposure." *Sierra,* 43–49, 76.

Tarshis, Lauren. "Dumping on Minorities." *Scholastic Update,* April 17, 1992, 16–17.

"Unequal Protection" (A Special Investigation). *National Law Journal,* September 24, 1992, Supplement 1–12.

Waldman, Steven, with Debra Rosenberg and Patrick Rogers. "Lead and Your Kids." *Newsweek,* July 15, 1991, 42–48

INDEX

128